Maybe all men got one big soul where everybody's
a part of — all faces of the same man:
one big self.

— Terrence Malick

"Hustleman" Transylvania, Louisiana

doc # 127809
dob. 8.17.76
pob. Shreveport
tattoo. *Naughty*
by Nature
Born Killer
ECPPF 1999

Angola, Louisiana

St. Gabriel, Louisiana

doc # 93665
dob. 6. 29. 63
pob. Florida
entered LSP. 1982
sentence.
41 years 9 months
work. metal fab.
rodeo event.
bulldoggin'
LSP 10. 31. 99

doc # 333265
dob. 11. 17. 71
pob. New Orleans
sentence. 1 year
3 children
work. outer perimeter
LCIW 3. 20. 00

St. Gabriel, Louisiana

James Lee Flowers Angola, Louisiana

doc # 227295
dob. 9. 15. 59
pob. Lafayette
sentence. 15 months
work. road crew
LCIW 6. 15. 00

doc # 98937
dob. 3. 21. 61
pob. New Orleans
entered LSP. 1984
sentence. LIFE
work. A & B Squad
LSP 3. 19. 99

Tyrone "Big" House Transylvania, Louisiana

Angola, Louisiana

doc # 431207

dob. 11. 21. 79

pob. Baton Rouge

sentence. 5 years

2 children

future plans. welding

ECPPF 3. 8. 02

doc # 368527

dob. 1. 26. 77

pob. Syracuse, NY

entered LSP. 1998

sentence. LIFE

work. grass crew

LSP 3. 19. 99

Kathy Wilford St. Gabriel, Louisiana

Peter Davis Angola, Louisiana

doc # 388348
dob. 9. 5. 67
pob. Antioch, CA
sentence. 2½ years
work. housekeeper
LCIW 6. 15. 00

doc # 90015
dob. 11. 25. 61
pob. New Orleans
entered LSP. 1987
sentence. LIFE
work. kitchen
LSP 3. 19. 99

John "Dead Eye" Hayes Transylvania, Louisiana

St. Gabriel, Louisiana

doc # 128997

dob. 3. 30. 66

pob. Shreveport

sentence. 2 years

2 children

future plans.

raise horses

ECPPF 6. 1. 00

doc # 302981

dob. 12. 07. 66

pob. Baton Rouge

sentence. 21 years

3 children

work. chair plant

LCIW 11. 30. 99

Tydia Powell St. Gabriel, Louisiana

Mitchell R. "Pops" Taylor Transylvania, Louisiana

doc # 335758
dob. 2. 16. 69
pob. New Orleans
sentence. 15 years
3 children
work. inner yard
Wearing a *"stand-by-
the-door* dress"
LCIW 7. 12. 00

doc # 293922
dob. 7. 12. 50
pob. Independence
sentence. 5 years
3 children
future plans.
landscaper
ECPPF 7. 15. 00

St. Gabriel, Louisiana

doc #166061
dob. 10. 10. 68
pob. New Orleans
sentence. 5 years
2 children
work. culinary arts
LCIW 4. 30. 99

One Big Self

Prisoners of Louisiana

Text + C.D. Wright

Photographs + Deborah Luster

Brenda Lathers St. Gabriel, Louisiana

Donald Garringer Angola, Louisiana

doc # 397017

dob. 6. 4. 76

pob. Baton Rouge

sentence. 3 years

4 children

work. field

LCIW 6. 20. 99

doc #115224

dob. 12. 31. 62

pob. D.Q.

entered LSP. 1990

sentence. LIFE

work. line 11

LSP 9. 17. 99

The Reappearance of Those Who Have Gone

by Deborah Luster ✝ Louisiana, 2002

Each Life Converges to some Centre —
Expressed — or still —

Emily Dickinson

In the 1950s and 60s, my grandmother, Mary Elizabeth Pyeatt Gunter, consistently and inadvertently produced a series of photographs, "the diagonal family." Each frame in this series from our family ark—full of cats, dogs, horses, and blood kin—appeared to list approximately ten degrees, as if taking on water. Later, my mother, Jean Alryn Gunter Tovrea, documented our annual Christmas trees, the evolution of our fashion sensibilities, and seemingly, our family's every mood and move. These, along with photographs taken long before my birth, were kept secure in several albums or haphazardly in an orange wooden box. In Arkansas, where I grew up, these photographs served as touchstones for the countless tellings of our family story. They described the history of our land, and our family's colorful characters and steady loss of fortune. The orange box was my favorite object for it contained hundreds of photographs, loose for the touching. For countless hours I would arrange and read the hypnotic language of the bodies and faces of my kin. Time and death dissolved when my great-grandfather and I stood side by side as slips of paper. I was in the here and now. I was in the there and then. I was neither here nor there. I was making contact. I was converging.

Perhaps I was channeling my ancestors in the years following the deaths of my mother and grandmother. Perhaps it was their spirits that moved me to pick up a camera—for in our family, the camera was manned by women. It was my turn. Or perhaps I picked up the camera out of desperation. I did need a tool. I was buried under the loss of my family members. The world was a sinister one. I was awake and numb and frightened. How could I sleep under the same stars as my mother's murderer? I used the camera to dig out. I found that I was still capable of making contact.

Nine years later, I stood in a courtroom following the conviction of the man hired to murder my mother. I looked around the room. Here sat the remnants of my family. There, across the aisle, sat the family of the convicted. So many lives destroyed or damaged by this greedy, stupid act. I wondered if there remained a single soul untouched by violence. Violence in the name of hatred and in the name of love; violence in the name of righteousness and the almighty buck. No contact.

In the fall of 1998 the Louisiana Endowment for the Humanities funded a group of photographers sent out to document the state's northeast parishes. I was one of those photographers driving around on Delta roads looking for inspiration. I was rounding a long curve and wondering where all the people were when I saw a small prison. Maybe this is where the people live, I thought. I parked the truck, got out, and knocked on the gate. Large birds circled high overhead. Warden Ray Dixon walked out of his office. "Fine with me," said the warden. I photographed at the East Carroll Parish Prison Farm. I developed and printed the portraits. Convergence.

Louisiana incarcerates more of its population than any other state in the Union. The United States incarcerates more of its population than any other country in the free world. For three and a half years I photographed at three Louisiana prisons.

East Carroll Parish Prison Farm at Transylvania was built in 1935. It is located a few miles from the Mississippi River in northeast Louisiana. It is a minimum-security parish facility housing approximately two hundred men. The majority of these men are state prisoners serving terms of under five years for drug possession or parole violations. No man at East Carroll is down for more than ten years. Seventy percent of the population is African American. Most of the men have completed less than nine years of formal education. A gymnasium, volleyball court, and iron pile are provided for physical recreation. A small chapel sits on the corner of the compound, where many of the men attend religious services on Sundays and weddings on Saturday mornings. There is a pond near the gate with ducks, fish, turtles, and snakes where the current warden and ordained minister, Edward Knight, conducts baptisms.

The Louisiana Correctional Institute for Women at St. Gabriel is a minimum-, medium-, and maximum-security facility housing approximately one thousand women. The prison is located a few miles from the Mississippi River in south Louisiana. The St. Gabriel facility more closely resembles a campus than a prison. The grounds are immaculate, and elaborate handmade decorations are rotated throughout the year to acknowledge the changing season's celebrations. The majority of inmates at St. Gabriel are serving sentences directly or indirectly related to drugs. Approximately 10 percent are serving life sentences, and there is one woman on Death Row. Over 39 percent of the women who entered St. Gabriel between 1995 and 2000 tested below the sixth-grade level. Approximately 65 percent of the prison population are African American. The guards at St. Gabriel, almost exclusively women, are not armed, and no gun is kept on the premises.

The Louisiana State Penitentiary at Angola is a maximum-security facility housing over five thousand men on eighteen thousand acres of Delta farmland. Angola once served as a slave-breeding farm and is surrounded on three sides by the Mississippi River. The topsoil here is purported to be twelve feet deep. Inmates work the fields (at a wage of between 4 and 8 cents per hour) that produce food for Angola and other correctional facilities around the state — four million pounds of vegetables per year. Cotton and feed crops are also grown. Fifteen hundred head of cattle and over two hundred horses are raised on this working plantation. Eighty-seven percent of Angola's inmates are violent offenders. Forty percent are first offenders. Seventy-eight percent of inmates are African American. The average inmate reads at the third-grade level. Angola's oldest inmate is ninety-one years old, and the youngest is seventeen. There are ninety men on Death Row. Eighty-eight percent of the men who are incarcerated at Angola will die there. Following the bombing of the World Trade Center on September 11th, Angola's inmate population donated $13,000 to aid victims of the disaster.

I cannot explain the need I felt to produce these portraits, because I do not fully understand it myself. I only know that it has something to do with the formal quality of loss and the way we cannot speak directly to those who have gone — how to touch the disappeared. I cannot explain my need to produce these portraits in such numbers except to say that I needed an aesthetic equivalent to the endless and indirect formality of loss. I also needed rules to support my intentions and to keep from being trapped by them.

Dorothea Lange said, "The best way to go into an unknown territory is to go in ignorant, as ignorant as possible, with your mind wide open, as wide open as possible not having to meet anyone else's requirements but your own." Before I started photographing inmates, I chose not to read accounts of prison life or study the numbing statistics. I wanted the portraits to be as direct a telling as possible — to hold up a mirror for the viewer as well as the subject. My hypostatic concerns required me to become a more disciplined, patient, hardworking, and contemplative photographer, and in some ways a less imaginative one.

We are all creatures of chance and choice. I chose to photograph each person as they presented their very own selves before my camera on the chance that I might be fortunate enough to contact, as poet Jack Gilbert writes, "their hearts in their marvelous cases." I took my chances. I wanted this to be as collaborative an enterprise as possible.

Each person photographed received an average of ten to fifteen wallet-sized prints. I have returned over twenty-five thousand prints to inmates. For the inmates and their families these photographs can be magic things in ways that a letter or a visit cannot be. One woman, whose nineteen children had not written or visited her in the fifteen years of her incarceration, wanted to send photos home to "soften the hearts" of her children. A few months later, four of her children came to St. Gabriel for a reunion with their mother, down for ninety-nine years. An Angola inmate sent his photos to his sister in Florida. She had not seen him in over thirty years. Contact.

An inmate at Angola called out to me on the walk, "You been to St. Gabriel, haven't you?" "How did you know that?" I answered. I had only just visited St. Gabriel for the first time a week or two before. He replied, "'Cause I sent my girlfriend that picture you took of me and she sent me back one just like it." The act of photographing and returning prints to these incarcerated persons and their eventual distribution of the portraits to friends and family are as important to this project, and compelling to me, as any formal exhibition or publication of the images.

The final portraits, like my family's photographs, are small enough to be held in the hand—five by four inches. They are printed on prepared black aluminum. Information supplied by the inmates is etched on the back of each plate and these plates are housed, loose, in a large black steel cabinet. To find the plates the viewer must pull open the heavy steel drawers that hold them. The plates may then be held and read or arranged on the cabinet top.

These photographs belong to the eyes of the free world viewer — citizen, voter, gallery goer, broker of social policy. They are intended to serve as a reminder of the thin blue line traced by societal and telluric forces that contribute so often to our personal fortunes. They belong equally to the eyes of the photographed in their own universe of family and friends, intended as evidence of life, presented here, as André Breton has written, not only as faces to be examined but also "as oracles to be questioned."

Artists, I believe, are often drawn by spirits into strange places. I found myself walking through prison gates. I felt the leaden hours of the forsaken and forgotten. I felt the certain slowing of time and thickening of space — neither here nor there. In this place I found it easy to believe that the earth came from a great swirl of gases and that someday it would end. I have come to understand that, while it was the fear and anger generated by my mother's murder that in great measure ignited this work, it is the loss and hope I feel—that we each feel, one and all—that has fueled it.

Annette Rose St. Gabriel, Louisiana

doc #391605
dob. 1. 31. 74
pob. New Orleans
sentence. 5 years
3 children
work. field
LCIW 6. 25. 99

One Big Self
by C.D. Wright

Larry Knighten Transylvania, Louisiana

"Juice" Angola, Louisiana

doc # 24873

dob. 11. 16. 63

pob. Baton Rouge

sentence. 3 years

transferred to

Ft. Wade Prison

Mental Health Unit

ECPPF 1998

doc # 360828

dob. 11. 8. 76

pob. Hart, MI

entered LSP. 1997

sentence. 12 years

work. A & B Squad

LSP 3. 19. 99

God was pleased by the good he did and we pray his mercy for the wrong— the lone epitaph at Point Lookout Cemetery, Angola. Charles C. Hawell, died in January, nineteen and thirty-four, at thirty-four years of age, and as stipulated in his will was brought back inside for burial after he was released.

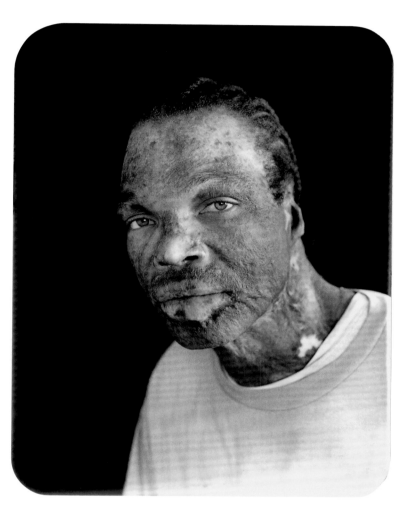

"Bolottie" Transylvania, Louisiana

Christina Kolozsvari St. Gabriel, Louisiana

doc # 337700

dob. 6. 19. 65

pob. Monroe

sentence. 8 ½ years

5 children

future plans.

self-employed

E C P P F 6. 1. 00

doc # 300079

dob. 10. 7. 64

pob. Canada

sentence. 5 years

3 children

work. outer perimeter

LCIW 6. 25. 99

Count your fingers

Count your toes

Count your nose holes

Count your blessings

Count your stars (lucky or not)

Count your loose change

Count the cars at the crossing

Count the miles to the state line

Count the ticks you pulled off the dog

Count your calluses

Count your shells

Count the points on the antlers

Count the newjack's keys

Count your cards; cut them again

Count heads. Count the men's. Count the women's. There are five main counts in the cell or work area. 4:45 first morning count. I/m must stand for the count. The count takes as long as it takes. Control Center knows how many should be in what area. No one moves from area A to area B without Control knowing. If i/m is stuck out for the count i/m receives a write up. Three write ups, and i/m goes to lockdown. Once

        in lockdown, you will relinquish your things:

plastic soapdish, jar of vaseline, comb or hairpick, paperback

        Upon return to your unit the inventory officer

will return your things:

        soapdish, vaseline, comb, hairpick, paperback

        Upon release you may have your possessions:

        soapdish, vaseline, comb, pick, book

Whereupon your True Happiness can begin

In the Mansion of Happiness:

Whoever possesses CRUELTY

Must be sent back to JUSTICE

Whoever gets into IDLENESS

Must come to POVERTY

Whoever becomes a SABBATHBREAKER

Must be taken to the Pillory

and there remain until he loses 2 turns

Betty "Sweet Black" Fullilove St. Gabriel, Louisiana

"Gumby" Angola, Louisiana

doc # 230341

dob. 5. 25. 49

pob. Mississippi

sentence. 4½ years

4 children

Work. Housekeeping

LCIW 11. 30. 99

doc # 102106

dob. 10. 23. 55

pob. Muskogee, OK

entered LSP. 1984

sentence. 40 years

work. range crew

rodeo events.

bull riding, bare back,

bust out, wild horse race

LSP 10. 31. 99

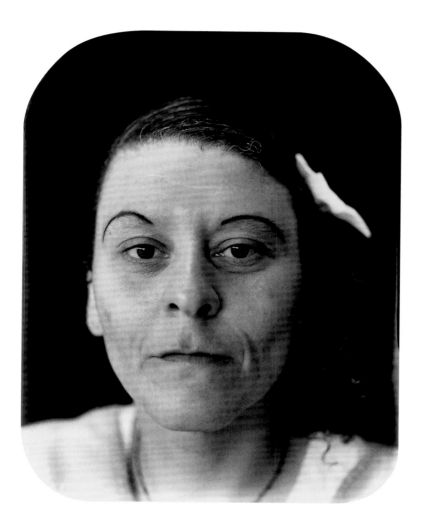

Christine Levy St. Gabriel, Louisiana

St. Gabriel, Louisiana

doc # 346225
dob. 10. 10. 59
pob. Lafayette
sentence. 10 years
work. chair plant
LCIW 4. 30. 99

doc # 318918
dob. 12. 10. 62
pob. New Orleans
sentence. 3 years
5 children
work. inner yard
LCIW 6. 15. 00

I want to go home, Patricia whispered.

I won't say I like being in prison, but I have learned a lot, and I like experiences. The terriblest part is being away from your families. — Juanita

I miss my screenporch.

I know every word to every song on *Purple Rain*. — Willie

I'm never leaving here. — Grasshopper, in front of the woodshop, posing beside a coffin he built.

This is a kicks' camp. Nothing positive come out of here except the praying. Never been around this many women in my life. Never picked up cursing before. — down for manslaughter, 40 years.

I've got three. One's seven. One, four. One, one. I'm twenty-three. The way I found out is, I was in an accident with my brother. He was looking at some boys playing ball. We had a head on.

At the hospital, the doctor says, Miss, why didn't you tell us you were pregnant. I'm pregnant? I wasn't afraid of my mama. I was afraid of my daddy. I was supposed to be a virgin. He took it real good though.

The last time you was here I had a headful of bees.

See what I did was, I accidentally killed my brother.

He spoke without inflection.

Asked how many brothers and sisters did he have —

On my mother's side, two brothers, well now, one brother, and two sisters. On my father's side, fifteen sisters.

When I handed Franklin his prints, his face broke.
Damn, he said to no one, *I done got old.*

                         I kept a dog.

When you walk through Capricorn, keep your arms down and close to your
    body.

                                  That's my sign.

No, she can't have no mattress. No, she can't have no spoon.
    See if she throwed her food yet.

                                  No, she can't have no more.
    I am only about thirty-four minutes from home. That's hard — George,
field line seated on a bag of peas on a flatbed.

    My auntie works here, and two of my cousins. If I get in trouble,
get a write up, my mama knows before supper. — George

    My name is Patricia, but my real name is Zabonia, she spoke softly.

Some have their baby and are brought back on the bus the next day and act like
it doesn't bother them a bit. Some cry all the way. And for days. — guard

                              That's hard.
                              I don't go there.

My mama was fifteen when she had me. That's common
                in the country.

                          Some can learn, and will be okay.
Some could stay in the class forever and not learn. S_ when she was a little girl
was struck in the head with a machete, and I don't think she'll learn much more....

She *is so* sweet. You wouldn't believe she had did all the things they say
        she did.

                                Don't ask.

My mug shot totally turned me against being photographed.

                                I miss the moon.
I miss silverware, with a knife,

                                and maybe even something to cut with it.

                                I miss a bathtub.
                                And a toilet. With a lid. And a handle.
                                And a door.

When Grasshopper came to Big Gola his wife was pregnant. He saw the baby once.
Next when he was 20. Now he's inside. In Texas. Second time. But he's short now.
He'll get out soon.

                                    That's hard.
                                    I don't go there.

                        I miss driving.

        We're both here because of love. —Zabonia of herself and her best friend

                        I am highly hypnotizable.

    I would wash that man's feet and drink the water.

Misty Buffington St. Gabriel, Louisiana

Joe Jackson Angola, Louisiana

doc # 347498

dob. 1. 18. 78

pob. Denver, CO

sentence. LIFE

work. horticulture

Halloween

Haunted House

LCIW 10. 27. 00

doc # 109666

dob. 9. 16. 59

pob. Independence

entered LSP. 1984

sentence. 3 LIFE

No Duty

DOD 7. 28. 99

LSP 3. 18. 99

Prison Hospital

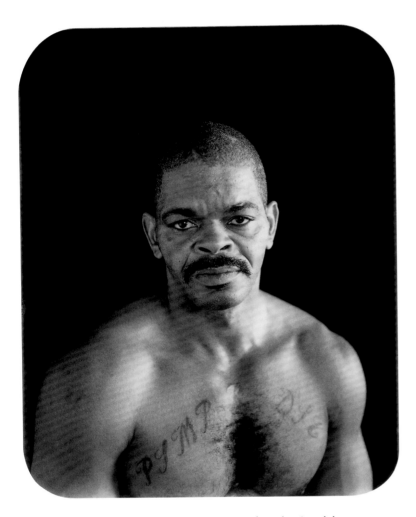

Samuel "Pimp" Lane, Jr. Transylvania, Louisiana

Johnny R. Collins Angola, Louisiana

doc # 113380

dob. 8. 9. 57

pob. New Orleans

sentence. 5 years

3 children

future plans. work

tattoo. PIMP R DIE

ECPPF 7. 13. 00

doc # 89196

dob. 8. 31. 52

pob. Shreveport

entered LSP. 1979

sentence. LIFE

work. tier walker

tattoo. Love is Hell

LSP 3. 19. 99

If I were you:

Screw up today, and it's solitary, Sister Woman, the padded dress with the food log to gnaw upon. This is where you enter the eye of the fart. The air is foul. The dirt is gumbo. Avoid all physical contact. Come nightfall the bugs will carry you off.

I don't have a clue, do I.

If you were me:

If you wanted blueberries you could have a big bowl. Two dozen bushes right on your hill. And thornless raspberries at the bottom. Walk barefooted; there's no glass. If you want to kiss your kid you can. If you want a Porsche, buy it on the installment plan. You have so many good books you can't begin to count them. Walk the dog to the bay every living day. The air is salted. Septembers you can hear the blues jumping before seeing water through the vault in the leaves. Watch the wren nesting in the sculpture by the shed. Smoke if you feel like it. Or swim. Call a friend. Or keep perfectly still. The mornings are free.

If I were a felon I'd be home now

Sandra Gilbert St. Gabriel, Louisiana

doc #130795
dob. 6. 30. 59
pob. Lafayette
sentence. 21 years
LCIW 6. 15. 00

Bienvenu en Louisiane

The septuagenarian murderer knits nonstop

One way to wear out the clock

In Tickfaw miracles occur

This weekend: the thirteenth annual Cajun joke contest

They will/will not be sending the former governor to Big Gola

I pinch a cigarette and stare at Rachel's wrist scars

By their color they are recent

That the eye not be drawn in

I suggest all courage is artificial

Her sister did not fail

Noses amuse us and hers not less so

     Short   smart   butch
Utterly unsure of herself

Whichever you see as sadder

A jukebox or a coffin

A woman's hand will close your eyes

On the surface she is receptive

I wear the lenses of my time
Some run to type, but I am not qualified

Hectored by questions that have to do with the Forms of Harm,
        the Nature of the Beast, Mercy, etc.

Last seen yesterday morning in a one-piece swimsuit

The popular sixteen-year-old is 5′7″, 127 lbs

The K-9 unit given her long white prom gloves, her pillowcase

Do you wish to save these changes
        yes   no   nevermind

The stinging caterpillars of Tickfaw pour onto the bark
        in the form of a cross

A random book skimmed from the women's shelf

In which an undine-like maiden
        is espyed feeding white daisies to a bear

Something on anarcho-syndicalism wasn't really expected

        poetry   time   space   death

Church marquee: AFTER GOOD FRIDAY COMES EASTER
                        GOD ALWAYS WINS

Drive-in marquee: Lenten Special
        poboys   fries   drink

The men pretty much all have ripped chests

Knitting wasn't really expected

Sign on the weight machine: PUSH TO FAILURE

Whoever becomes a DRUNKARD must be taken to the Whipping Post

Dino's out, he'd like his pictures
Dino blowing smoke out the holes of his beautiful nose

Wilhemina Joseph St. Gabriel, Louisiana

Felton Williams Angola, Louisiana

doc # 98152

dob. 3. 26. 55

pob. New Orleans

sentence. 50 years

2 children

work.

office occupations

LCIW 4. 30. 99

doc # 73308

dob. 11. 21. 38

pob. Edgard, LA

entered LSP. 1972

sentence. LIFE

work. orderly

member. Angola Senior

Citizens Club

LSP 3. 17. 99

She is *so* sweet you wouldn't believe she had did
  all the things they say she did

That one, she's got a gaggle of tricks up her you know what

Drawn on a wall in solitary by a young one
  MOM LOVE GOD
  before he had a face on him

Don't blink don't miss nothing: It's *your* furlough

The Asian lady beetle won't reproduce indoors

The missing girl's father is a probation officer

Do you want to download this
  now later no comment

Solitary confinement, Mr. Abbott wrote,
  can alter the ontological makeup of a stone

Mr. Abbott was state-raised, he knows

Zero% financing and drive-through daiquiris

Baggies of hair and nail clippings entered in

You can bet your nickels

The former 4-term governor will be well-lawyered

What is *your problem*

The tier walker checks on the precariously living

Photographed him with a boner

That's not my pencil, is it

Check his prints:
  plain tented looped burned off

It is a stock dog, the state dog, catahoula
      with the rain-blue eyes

Church marquee: LET'S MEET AT MY HOUSE BEFORE THE GAME

Lead (kindly) light   Enter (softly) evil

Ebony Ellis St. Gabriel, Louisiana

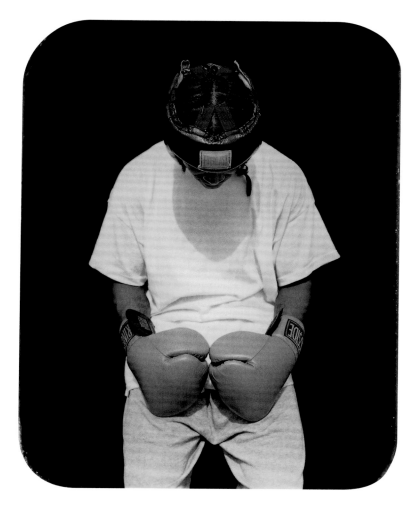

Daniel "Juvnile" Smith Angola, Louisiana

doc # 366050
dob. 3. 22. 73
pob. New Orleans
sentence. 10 years
3 children
work. inner yard,
tablecloth ironer
Halloween
Haunted House
LCIW 10. 27. 00

doc # 130584
dob. 10. 9. 73
pob. New Orleans
work. field
sentence. LIFE
LSP 6. 10. 99

Earl Crum Angola, Louisiana

doc # 112063

dob. 9 . 23 . 59

pob. Baton Rouge

entered LSP. 1994

sentence. LIFE

work. librarian

LSP 6 . 10 . 99

St. Gabriel, Louisiana

doc # 298170
dob. 7. 26. 68
pob. New Orleans
sentence. 7 years
4 children
work. chair plant
Halloween
Haunted House
LCIW 10. 27. 00

My Dear Conflicted Reader,

If you will grant me that most of us have an equivocal nature, and that when we waken we have not made up our minds which direction we're headed; so that — you might see a man driving to work in a perfume-and-dye-free shirt, and a woman with an overdone tan hold up an orange flag in one hand, a Virginia Slim in the other — as if this were their predestination. Grant me that both of them were likely contemplating a different scheme of things. WHERE DO YOU WANT TO SPEND ETERNITY the church marquee demands on the way to my boy's school, SMOKING OR NON-SMOKING. I admit I had not thought of where or which direction in exactly those terms. The radio ministry says g-o-d has a wrong-answer button and we are all waiting for it to go off....

Count your grey hairs

Count your chigger bites

Count your pills

Count the times the phone rings

Count your T cells

Count your mosquito bites

Count the days since your last menses

Count the chickens you've eaten

Count your cankers

Count the storm candles

Count your stitches

Count your broken bones

Count the flies you killed before noon

Morgan Ezell Angola, Louisiana

Brian "Lil' Collins" Jackson Transylvania, Louisiana

doc #324750
dob. 9. 20. 68
pob. Louisiana
entered. 1994
sentence. 35 years
work. pre-release exit program
rodeo events.
bulldoggin', wild cow milking
1999 Convict Poker Champion
LSP 10. 31. 99

dob. 2. 6. 79
pob. Ruston
sentence. 8 years
future plans.
own a barber shop
ECPPF 1999

Jacob Crawford Transylvania, Louisiana

St. Gabriel, Louisiana

doc. #411034
dob. 8.15.55
pob. New Orleans
ECPPF 1999

doc # 411034
dob. 10.14.75
pob. Detroit, MI
sentence. 5 years
2 children
work. chair plant
Mardi Gras Parade
LCIW 3.2.01

                                        On the road to Angola:

                    Handmade sign: bullwhips
                    Turn-off: Solitude, Louisiana
                    Property Gate: West Inheritance

                                        On the road to St. Gabriel:

Zipping through Ferriday   Great Balls o' Fire
            If it ain't The Killer's hometown

In the old days they would have sent you to America

The one called Grasshopper raises wild things — sparrows, hares, you name it

They've got a muleskinner here that can make one sit down and talk

Then there's the wren nesting in the razor wire

I read that the former governor is employing Mr. Von Bulow's attorney

Sissy is Mr. Redwine's catahoula

Nolan knows where the dove eggs are

Pop named every single one of his roses, his company keepers

I haven't found anyone good enough for my cats, said Lyles

He bottle-fed the colt Lil Tête, and rehabilitated Ginger
        whose backend is sunken still

That dog, the guard said, is emancipated
That man, Nolan said, of Ginger's former keeper
        Didn't need no dog

Smurf is photographed with Daisy; she' just a pup

But she's a filia brazilia
        as draft horse to regular horse, the very core of horseness

Tiger Lady, Storm, Kilo, Thunder, Josie, Duke, Bonnie, Blaze,
        Dolly, Grubby, Jack, Buster, Tracker

        Put your hands together for the K-9 unit

If they can get outside the fence they still have to beat the dogs
        No one's beat the dogs yet, said Castlebury

Whoever possesses AUDACITY must be taken to the Water
        and thoroughly ducked

Swallows multiply in the Red Hat building

The greenhouse dog is Fancy

In the Red Hat building Old Sparky gathers webs

No condoms for the heart

Violence, H. Rap Brown proclaimed, is American as apple pie

Over 6 trillion served; over 2 million behind bars

Mr. Redwine is the coffin builder; Grasshopper his apprentice

Built a replica of Old Sparky for the prison museum

International Harvester provided the generator for the original
        drove it around on a flatbed
        from penitentiary to penitentiary

About the thickness of a pair of panties, Your Honor
        She was a slab of a woman

The radio calls it predatory selection,
        as in white sharks' preference for seals

Her husband, he was a wonderful, wonderful man

That one, he should have never been born
Some run to type

To be a good host the Christian DJ in the Dale Carnegie T-shirt
      offers us a cup of tepid kool-aid

To be a good guest we lift our cups and drink
      I have a petty fear of red

Where I come from the guest must honor her host

                            Notice: Camp J
                            Due to religious call-out No band call-out

Mural of the Last Supper, call-out building, east wall

What is that the disciples are eating do you think
      crawfish   chicken   gar

      when the Muslims bow to the east

      the mural covered with corduroy

Every faith allowed except Satanism

Wall plaque:
      This is to certify that Bloodhound Site
      Was entered into the National Register of Historical Places
      National Preservation Act of 1966

Her inamorato, he was a wonderful, wonderful man

That one, he was an inveterate pig

                        DUE TO THEFT:
                All True Crime and Black Study titles
                Are housed in closed shelving
                Limit 3 books per person
                O exceptions   so don't ask

Pamela Winfield St. Gabriel, Louisiana

doc # 312197
dob. 11. 25. 64
pob. N. Kingston, RI
sentence. 5 years
work. floor worker
Easter Bunny
Children's Visiting Day
LCIW 4. 14. 00

Saturday night
Going to Walmart
Satisfaction guaranteed

Over six trillion served, two million put away

It gets old   the way we do things

And Nolan is the Buddha
Maybe   Maybe not

His mansuetude manifest

No one here for walking on the grass

On the road to St. Gabriel:

The highest concentration of makers and dumpers
Of toxic chemicals in the country   and 7th on the planet
known locally and globally as Cancer Alley

Described herself as a shy bible-reading woman
That one, don't make me laugh

I tell you what she knows now, she knows
        le ciel est par-dessus le toit

She knows NOTHING AND NO ONE IS BAD FOREVER

An old lover punched out a wall for a window in architecture
        this is known as a dream hole

On furlough   contemplate the grasses
        don't blink   don't miss nothing

He would finish his pie later he said, in all sincerity, over his last meal:
        poboy   fries   drink

A rattlesnake can bite up to sixty minutes after being decapitated
      that's how long its reflexes remain functional

      He did not say Let's Do It
      He said *dominicus vobiscum*

Lingers the implication that Gilmore's father
      was the bastard son of Houdini

There will come a time that he will move; he will have to move, and it is his
      movement that will be his undoing, said Castlebury

My ode to the double negative

Hell yes it's bitter, every bit of it bitter

      Et cum spiritu tuo

Constance Daugherty St. Gabriel, Louisiana

Bonita Jethro St. Gabriel, Louisiana

doc # 413776

dob. 7. 23. 74

pob. Franklinton

sentence. 4 years

4 children

work. culinary arts

cake decoration

LCIW 4. 14. 00

doc # 339855

dob. 12. 27. 67

pob. St. Louis, MO

sentence. 5 years

2 boys

work. culinary arts

LCIW 4. 30. 99

On Privacy

On the phone he told his sister
He hung strips of a plastic bag from his bunk
And pretended he was in his boat
And his cellmate's flushing, Arctic Ocean

On The Lessening of Free World Ties

The caller can see the phone
ringing in its cradle; see the light pour to the tiled floor, the magazines
heaped by the door, the old zinnias in a pepper jar, the leftovers,
the dog's bowl, the unread letters; can almost make out the handwriting;
almost certain it is her own

The men like *The Young and The Restless*

Some of us be rootin' for the bad guys; some of us be rootin' for the good — George

And some of us just be rootin'— from the turnrow

The women like *The Guiding Light*

The women like Nora Roberts and John Le Carré

The men like Danielle Steele and Louis L'Amour

Ever'body likes Jackie Collins

The men's units are named for animals and trees

They keep the young ones in Eagle
                    until they get a face on them

        The women's units are named for signs of the zodiac, Capricorn
is lockdown

                            That's my sign

She misses her clematis he misses his dogs

What they hold in common, their poverty

More than cold I dislike heat. If the Governor would release me to Alaska, I would promise never again to come anywhere near this state for any reason whatsoever

Favorite body of water: Arctic Ocean

My idea of a good car: anything that is fast, solid, and bullet-proofed

I can identify: Queen Caseopea (can't spell her name), Orion's belt, the Dippers, Seven Sisters

I detest okra —Willie

Wallace Istre Angola, Louisiana

Ronny "Ron Jon" Holmes Transylvania, Louisiana

doc #96415
dob. 12. 2. 60
pob. Lafayette
entered LSP. 1982
sentence. LIFE
work. kitchen
LSP 3. 19. 99

doc # 366568
dob. 7. 25. 70
pob. Maryville
sentence. 4 years
ECPPF 1999

My Dear Affluent Reader,

Welcome to the Pecanland Mall. Sadly, the pecan grove had to be dozed to build it. Home Depot razed another grove. There is just the one grove left and the creeper and the ivy have blunted its sun. The uglification of your landscape is all but concluded. We are driving around the shorn suburb of your intelligence, the photographer and her factotum. Later we'll walk in the shadows of South Grand. They say, in the heyday of natural gas, there were houses with hinges of gold. They say so. We are gaining on the cancerous alley of our death. Which, when all is said or unsaid, done or left undone, shriven or unforgiven, this business of dying, is our most commonly held goal.

Ready or not. O exceptions.

Don't ask.

Prepare to exit the forest   of men and women

Louisiana bumper sticker: Jesus Don't Leave Earth Without Us

It's a great day to die, a great day to leave the body, he told the press
       before his Easter execution

When I go, I want my lips smythe-sewn, none of that perfect-bound crap
       it doesn't last

And burn me up I don't want any more real estate

No one promised you the light   or the morrow

Mother Helen predicts you will be doing better moneywise
       between March and May

In your past life you had something to do with animals
       she sees you in a hospital with animals way back in the 1800s

After all, you are not Gramsci, she said

Qui facit per alium facit per se

Sounds dirty doesn't it

I wanted to offer you the bread of charity,

Mercy, etc.

When she said she would write the book
       he said what direction

Take this down, then burn it

My faulty eschatology   pardon my french

The lovebugs   hitting the windshield like something electric
Jack and Jill the pastor at St. Gabriel calls them

Wonderful news   Sissy had seven little catahoulas
       Mr. Redwine in ecstasy

Amanda Webb St. Gabriel, Louisiana

doc #131329

dob. 2.24.71

pob. Shreveport

sentence. 21 years

LCIW 5.20.99

Denise Williams St. Gabriel, Louisiana

doc #294649
dob. 5.8.68
pob. New Orleans
sentence. 7 years
5 children
LCIW 5.28.99

James Lee Flowers Angola, Louisiana

Bobbie Johnson St. Gabriel, Louisiana

doc #98937
dob. 3.2.61
entered LSP. 1984
sentence. LIFE
work. A & B Squad
LSP 6.11.99

doc #88043
dob. 11.5.56
pob. New Orleans
sentence. LIFE
3 children
work. chair plant
Mardi Gras Parade
Honor Court
LCIW 3.2.01

Dear Dying Town,

The food is cheap; the squirrels are black; the box factories have all moved offshore; the light reproaches us, and our coffee is watered down, but we have an offer from the Feds to make nerve gas; the tribe is lobbying hard for another casino; the bids are out to attract a nuclear dump; and there's talk of a supermax—

In the descending order of your feelings

Please identify your concerns

PS: Remember Susanville, where Restore the Night Sky has become the town cry.

Dialing Dungeons for Dollars
Prison Realty

publicly traded

          on the New York Stock Exchange under the symbol P Z N

The good news is:

Corrections Corporation of America increased its inmate mandays by 12% From 15.1 million in 1998 to 16.9 million in 1999   A manday is one inmate held for one day for which the company bills government a *per diem* The increase in mandays in 1999 led to a 19% increase in C C A's revenues for the year to $787 million

      Then there is Wackenhut Wackenhut Wackenhut Wackenhut

                               underwritten by Prudential Securities

Gary Faley Angola, Louisiana

doc # 291617

dob. 12. 23. 72

pob. Baton Rouge

entered L S P. 1992

sentence. LIFE

work. kitchen

L S P 3. 18. 99

prison hospital

Transylvania, Louisiana

doc # 360751
dob. 9.18.76
pob. Knoxville, TN
1 child
sentence. 5 years
tattoo. Fuck You
ECPPF 5.24.01

James Willis Transylvania, Louisiana

George Georgetown Transylvania, Louisiana

doc #394655
dob. 7. 27. 77
pob. Ruston
ECPPF 1999

doc #260593
dob. 6. 28. 63
pob. Baton Rouge
sentence. 5 years
ECPPF 6. 3. 00

Modern Times

have seen a new spirit come over the peace agencies engaged in the war on crime. This spirit rose with the entrance of Finger Print Science into the battle.

You've got your plain loops, plain arches, tented arches, twin loops, lateral pocket loops, central pocket loops, whorls, and your accidentals

Found: his nineteen-year-old testicles
         in a bag in the river

How can that be shriven

Found: fourth body of a woman
         in a barrel

The man in the middle is Jesus

Bullets from a sawed off gun fan out faster

170 tablets of Ecstasy
         What if it's the drugs, Stupid

Than those from unmodified guns

Stippling is mostly confined to a 2-3 foot distance

How can that be shriven

Had taken to smoking 5 to 10 blunts a day

Water with a stomach wound is fatal

A jacketed bullet drives faster than a lead bullet

Well what do you know
         The former governor has employed Von Bulow's lawyer

People are bummed about the gag order

Just another miracle at Tickfaw

The pretty one from Natchitoches, her son is three;
      she has not seen him for a year and a half

                                That's hard

Powder tattooing, that's close range fire, leaves a circular pattern
      of black residue

The pretty one, that does hair, her son is two,
      she's a natural lifer
                        That's hard
      MOM   LOVE   GOD

Stacked blonde with sexy facial cicatrix

Wants the photos for her portfolio

You should see her cakes
      Esp. the one of the crucifixion

He was pronounced dead at 8:06 pm
She was pronounced dead at 8:16 pm
        one solitary day after their 14th wedding anniversary

BE JUST: inscription made by the harrow

Pour all the blood back into the earth

A woman's hand will close your eyes

Transfiguration kicks in

The red ribbon is for AIDS counseling

Pink for breast cancer counseling

The field line is wearing sombreros this year

The women like *The Guiding Light*

       him: 3 jolts in 2 minutes and 45 seconds
       her: 5 jolts, 4 minutes and 30 seconds

Orange is field line; Sky Blue is custom sewing

No one's beat the dogs yet, said Castlebury

Cigarettes still coin of the realm;
      at summer camp, it's beef jerky

The warden took a Butterfinger from one of the escapees,
      ate half of it in front of him; fed the rest to the pack leader

Sebastian Melmoth, Wilde's pseudonym upon release
      but he was pretty much finished with literature by then

Who felt chosen to teach
      the meaning of sorrow and its beauty

      that is literature was pretty much finished with Wilde

AC or DC
      You want to be westinghoused or edisoned
      Your pick   you're the one condemned

      Tennessee's retired chair available on E-Bay

Caravaggio, his *Deposition of Christ* (1604)
      a revolutionary use of light

      murdered his tennis partner

      for whatever it's worth

My friend here no longer sleeps in her own bed in
      her own house by her own self

The Heisenberg principle applies

      you change what you observe

Angola, Louisiana

Sheryl Knox St. Gabriel, Louisiana

doc # 87993

dob. 10. 5. 55

pob. Liberty MS

entered LSP. 1978

sentence. 33 years

work. carpenter

LSP 2. 24. 99

doc # 337933

dob. 11. 9. 63

sentence. 10 years

3 children

photo. 3. 2. 01

Angola, Louisiana

Artallic D. Wiley St. Gabriel, Louisiana

doc # 98923

dob. 7. 18. 42

pob. Boswell, OK

entered L S P. 1980

sentence. LIFE

work. clerk

L S P 2. 24. 99

doc # 406755

dob. 12. 5. 72

pob. New Orleans

sentence. 2 years

3 children

work. unit 3

L C I W 6. 25. 99

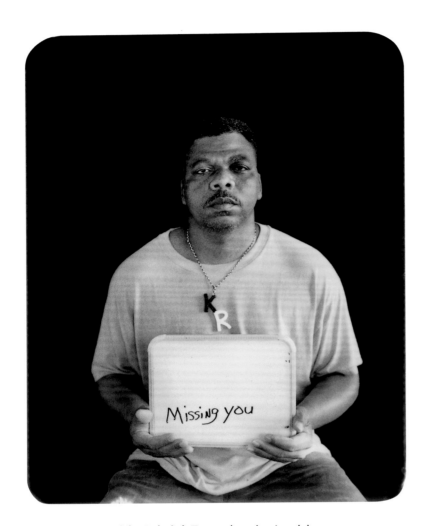

Keith Gabriel Transylvania, Louisiana

doc # 110182
dob. 7. 8. 61
pob. Independence
sentence. 33 months
4 children
future plans. work
ECPPF 7. 15. 00

Eddie M. "Fat" Coco, Jr. Transylvania, Louisiana

doc # 409584
dob. 6. 30. 79
pob. New Orleans
sentence. 6 years
children 2
future plans.
be success, lawyer
ECPPF 6. 1. 00

Dennis Leger Angola, Louisiana

doc # 71846
dob. 8. 25. 51
pob. Lafayette
entered LSP. 1969
sentence. LIFE
work. special squad
LSP 3. 19. 99

Did you ever do anything illegal
      maybe   maybe not   depends on your definition of legal

Who you going to believe me or my lying eyes

The goal is to transcend the course taken by blood
      color-coded authority   paternal cruelty

All these days I've been off death row
      death row has not been off me
                    the words of an exonerated man
Amaranthus, love lies bleeding to death
                  they call the summer poinsettia

Black is the Color

Of that big old ugly hole

Of 77% of the inmates in Angola

Of your true love's hair

Of 66% of the inmates at St. Gabriel

Of the executioner's corduroy hood

hung on an ice hook

in the tool shed

away from the kids

Wednesdays were important for Faith
            graduation day   active duty day   death day

Just to breathe   said the mother of Faith   the first year   an ordeal

It says foot for foot and burn for burn

        Mercy Triumphs Over Judgment
        as the saint would have it

I know that, and I know *Le ciel est par-dessus le toit,*
        Mais apres tout, I'm not Verlaine

Bound her hands with electrical cord, the young mother of 3

Stabbed her, the young mother, 23 times, took her wedding ring

How can that be shriven

White is kitchen; Burnt Pink is night floor technician;
        inner yard, Forest Green

The suspect was 9

I said I'm all stirred up

Come nearer
        where death hangs on its solitary hook in the shed

Your sentence, not a metonymy for our sins

Me, I'm Catholic so I was born guilty

I've always had the willies

Today it is hot as blue blazes and tonight it is going to be
        very very warm

Tomorrow it's going to be hot as blue blazes and tomorrow night
        very very warm

Precious Constance St. Gabriel, Louisiana

doc # 394693
dob. 9. 18. 76
pob. New Orleans
sentence. 1 year
4 children
work. floor worker
LCIW 4. 30. 99

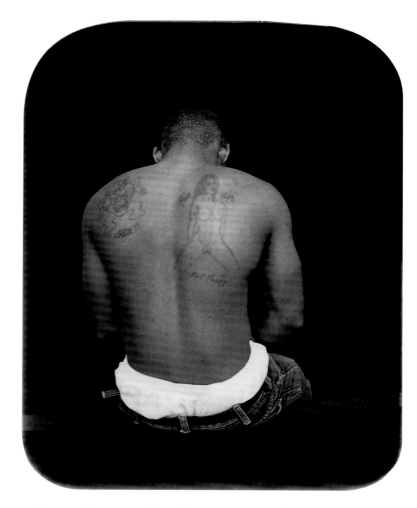

Steven Dewayne "Smurf" Turner Transylvania, Louisiana

doc #346251

dob. 1. 21. 76

tattoo: Hell!!

Real Men Eat Pussy

ECPPF 1999

Jenar Jury St. Gabriel, Louisiana

James Wells Angola, Louisiana

doc # 403946
dob. 10. 18. 62
pob. New Orleans
sentence. 3 years
6 children
work. computer, graphic artist,
boilermaker apprentice
LCIW 6. 15. 00

doc # 345585
dob. 7. 30. 76
pob. Franklin
entered LSP. 1996
sentence. 25 years
Angola "Cobras"
boxing team member
Boxing Extravaganza 2001
Light-Middleweight Crown
LSP 4. 22. 99

The women pass around a handmirror and a tube of lipstick
        they sit on the slab walk, smoke and talk

They pass a stuffed bunny from hand to hand
        for their turn in front of the camera

The church ladies are out on soul patrol
        they've got ditty bags for the prisoners

                                        Poster: Black History Month, women's prison
                                                The blacker the college
                                                The sweeter the knowledge

Navy is housekeeping,
Khaki is for peer tutor

The search for Molly is forty-five days old

If you were a felon
        you'd be home now

                                        Cradle my head Sister

        until the last rivet of grief is secure

                                        Why has the field line started so late

                                        Why does the light reproach us

                                        Why is the coffee so watered down

                                        What does it say on your blue sheet

                                        What will you lose if you stay

                                        What is your baby's name

Dear Unbidden, Unbred,

This is a flock of sorrows, of unoriginal sins, a litany of obscenities. This is a festering of hateful questions. Your only mirror is one of stainless steel. The image it affords will not tell whether you are young still or even real. In a claustral space. Hours of lead, air of lead. The sound, metallic and amped. You will know the force of this confinement as none other. You have been sentenced for worth-lessness. In other eyes, crucifixion is barely good enough. The strapdown team is on its way. The stricken, whose doves you harmed, will get a mean measure of peace. The schadenfreudes, the sons of schadenfreudes, will witness your end with "howls of execration." Followed by the burning of your worthless body on a pile of old tires. None will claim your remains nor your worthless effects: soapdish, vaseline, comb, paperback. All you possess is your soul whose mold you already deformed. You brought this on yourself. You and no one else. You with the dirty blonde hair, backcountry scars and the lazy dog-eye. You shot the law and the law won. You become a reject of hell.

Prison towns prison motels prison movies prison books prison dreams

    Voices in the air conditioning

    Convict hate convict sweat convict voices in the toilet tank

    This cell your dwelling; this grave your garden

Yolanda Banks St. Gabriel, Louisiana

Maureen Oubre St. Gabriel, Louisiana

doc #128877

dob. 10. 2. 58

pob. New Orleans

sentence. 5 years

2 children

work. kitchen

Halloween

Haunted House

LCIW 10. 27. 00

doc #388646

dob. 3. 15. 68

pob. Marrero

sentence. 5 years

1 child

work. vo-tech sewing

Halloween

Haunted House

"Electrocuted" Inmate

LCIW 10. 27. 00

Geraldine Washington St. Gabriel, Louisiana

DeMars Sisters St. Gabriel, Louisiana

doc # 419988
dob. 5.1.76
pob. New Orleans
sentence. 5 years
work. housekeeper
Halloween
Haunted House
LCIW 10.27.00

doc # 418257
dob. 8.10.79
pob. Baton Rouge
sentence. 2 ½ years
work. kitchen

doc # 380304
dob. 4.4.77
pob. Baton Rouge
sentence. 2 ½ years
5 children
work. inner yard
Halloween
Haunted House
LCIW 10.27.00

Denise Howard St. Gabriel, Louisiana

Jessie Hill St. Gabriel, Louisiana

doc #357771

dob. 10.7.65

pob. New Orleans

sentence. 3 years

1 child

no work

Halloween

Haunted House

LCIW 10.27.00

doc #113190

dob. 10.13.61

pob. New Orleans

sentence. 10 years

5 children

work. road crew

Halloween

Haunted House

LCIW 10.27.00

Tammy Mullins St. Gabriel, Louisiana

St. Gabriel, Louisiana

doc #372143
dob. 5.4.75
pob. Baton Rouge
sentence. 52 years
work. housekeeping
Mardi Gras Parade
LCIW 3.2.01

doc # 89930
dob. 3.5.42
pob. Cincinnati, OH
sentence. 60 years
4 children
work. upholstery, tutor
Mardi Gras Parade
Honor Court
LCIW 3.2.01

Joyce Murphey St. Gabriel, Louisiana

Concita Dixon St. Gabriel, Louisiana

doc # 353510

dob. 8. 2. 54

pob. New Orleans

sentence. 7 years

3 children

work. floors

Mardi Gras Parade

LCIW 3. 2. 01

doc # 271189

dob. 5. 23. 68

pob. Bossier City

2 children

sentence. LIFE

work. inner yard

Halloween

Haunted House

LCIW 10. 27. 00

Zelphea Adams St. Gabriel, Louisiana

doc # 404954
dob. 12. 19. 71
pob. New Orleans
sentence. 25 years
3 children
work. housekeeping
Mardi Gras Parade
LCIW 3. 2. 01

Michael "Lil' Red" Martin Angola, Louisiana

doc # 117260
dob. 2. 13. 62
pob. New Orleans
entered L S P. 1992
sentence. LIFE
work. laundry
LSP 6. 10. 99

Mack trapped a spider

Kept in a pepper jar

He named her Iris

Caught roaches to feed her

He loved Iris

When Iris died

He wrote her a letter

Dear night dear shade dear executioner

Fears: snakes   madness   falling

The sword has broken over this head

It sure enough gets old
the way we do things

Defend me   if you can
Collect my tears   if you will

G-o-d is the boss with the sauce

                he's too sweet to be sour

He's got his finger on the wrong answer button

                The ineffable joys for those who
unfeignedly love, transcend the documentary constraints,
      pledge mercy, etc.

After all, you are not Mandelstam

She said she was in love with Aqua Man
                Aqua Man?
                It's a shower head, Stupid

And that Sister Woman,   is what you call safe sex

    For whatever it's worth
135,000 take guns to school every day

Sound of that emotional collision
      between perps and victims

    No condoms for the heart

Donald Till Angola, Louisiana

doc # 340204

dob. 1. 31. 75

pob. Monroe

entered LSP. 1999

sentence. 6 years

work. line 1

LSP 6. 11. 99

Clarence "Lil' Daddy" Henderson Angola, Louisiana

Matthew Haynes Angola, Louisiana

doc # 95583
dob. 12. 27. ?
pob. New Orleans
entered LSP. 1981
sentence. LIFE
work. field
LSP 9. 17. 99

doc # 312754
dob. 1. 29. 71
pob. New Orleans
entered LSP. 1994
sentence. LIFE
work. line 1
LSP 6. 11. 99

Troy Knight Angola, Louisiana

Peter Lemm Angola, Louisiana

doc # 356098
dob. 3. 23. 73
pob. Baton Rouge
entered LSP. 1996
sentence. LIFE
work. cell block orderly
LSP. 6. 10. 99

doc # 116372
dob. 5. 9. 55
pob. Baton Rouge
entered LSP. 1986
sentence. LIFE
work. major's office
rodeo event.
guts and glory
LSP 10. 31. 99

Dear Prisoner,

        I too love.   Faces.   Hands.   The circumference
Of the oaks.   I confess.   To nothing
You could use.   In a court of law.   I found.
That sickly sweet ambrosia of hope.   Unmendable
Seine of sadness.   Experience taken away.
From you.   I would open.   The mystery
Of your birth.   To you.   I know.   We can
Change. Knowing.   Full well.   Knowing.
                                        It is not enough.
        Poetry   Time   Space   Death
I thought.   I could write.   An exculpatory note.
I cannot. Yes, it is bitter.   Every bit of it, bitter.
The course taken by blood.   All thinking
Deceives us.   Lead (kindly) light.
Notwithstanding this grave. Your garden.
This cell.   Your dwelling.   Who is unaccountably free.

No one promised you the light   or the morrow

                                        Poster, women's prison:
                                        Parts of Speech Fair
                                        Interjection, a word
                                        that expresses strong feeling
                                        UGH! WOW! OH!

                                        His last word: Wow
That's all he said, the warden told the camera

Mitterrand last dined on ortolans
        in the tradition of French kings
Some have crawfish with the warden; some dine on oxygen

In some prisons the last cigarette is no longer permitted
        O exceptions   Don't ask

An eye for an eye   it says in Exodus
Whose eye?
An eye

Audible light   an assault

The perimeter lined with summer poinsettias

Nieman Marcus has begun its Christmas countdown

                                Poster, prison greenhouse:
                                we guarantee our plants to grow
                                or die trying
Amaranthus:

        a.. An imaginary flower that never fades
        b.. A frequenter of prisons
        c.. To beat a spider to death with a broom

Foot for foot
burn for burn it says here

BE JUST — the inscription made by the harrow on the backfat and bone

Detric "D" Linear Transylvania, Louisiana

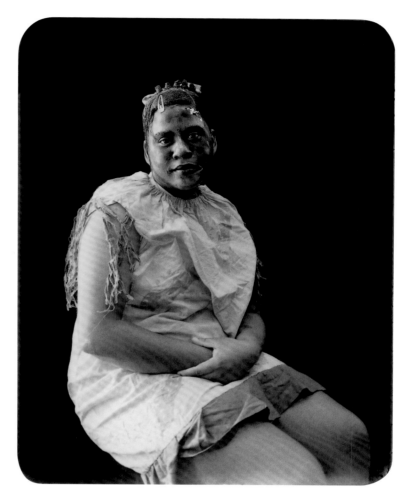

St. Gabriel, Louisiana

doc # 367866
dob. 11. 21. 77
pob. Shreveport
sentence. 18 months
tattoo. Blood Bunny
ECPPF 1999

doc # 391168
dob. 8. 10. 78
pob. Tallulah
sentence. 40 years
work. inner yard
Halloween
Haunted House
Alligator Girl
LCIW 10. 27. 00

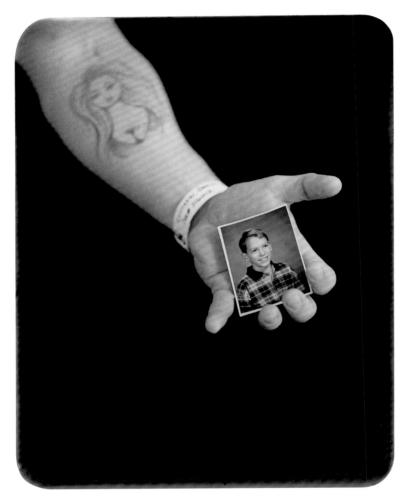

Transylvania, Louisiana

doc # 216042

dob. 7. 23. 70

pob. New Orleans

sentence.

3 ½ years

ECPPF 1999

St. Gabriel, Louisiana

doc # 335957
dob. 8. 23. 63
pob. Mississippi
sentence. 4 years
3 children
work. housekeeping
LCIW 6. 15. 00

                    Count your notches

                    Count your condoms before you go out

                              Saturday night
                              Satisfaction guaranteed

                    Count your folding money

                    Count the times you said you wouldn't go back

                    Count your debts

                    Count the roaches when the light comes on

                    Count your kids after the housefire

                    Count your cousins on your mother's side

                    Count your worrisome moles

                    Count your dead:

Dostoyevsky's epilepsy worsened after the mock execution

I saw children in the dirt yard   children in the sprinkler
Buckets of children   jumping through snatches of smoke

I saw a quivering dog in front of a quivering body of water
        his backend sunken still

I saw a cloud of lovebugs collect over the boxwood

        which smells like cat piss

        and the trillium that smells like skanky underwear
Dostoyevsky's father so frigging nasty, brutish and short
        murdered by his serfs

And something Cioran penned, I can't get out of my head
        No one can keep his griefs in their prime;
                              they use themselves up

Wherever you lay a dead snake its mate comes to lie with him

And another thing: Nothing And No One Is Bad Forever —Willie

People get jealous
      not a damn thing you can do about it, she told me privately

      Mother/daughter fall partners
      Did they cook the books or what
                            Don't ask
Nobody here for spitting on the sidewalk

I am the seventh child of Sister Rose. She put her life in JEOPARDY to come see
      about her son Aaron. A God-sent woman, born with the double veil, foresight

Wherever you find knots of men
you will find the charisma of violence

American as pie
      Poetry   Time   Space   Death
Leaving Transylvania   light yet

A gaggle of teens in front of the E-Z Mart   the one with dollar bills
pinned to his T-shirt is Dino's baby brother

Is it really your birthday or are you just fooling
    Mom   Love   God

                        Lake Providence
Last town in America to get rotary phones
town under curfew
                        New Town
The real real poor part of Lake Providence

Warden, Louisiana, other side of Epps

Epps Industrial Park: West Carroll Detention Center; that's it for industry

Frank "4 Watches" Joseph Angola, Louisiana

St. Gabriel, Louisiana

doc # 108325
dob. 11. 16. 48
pob. New Orleans
entered L.S.P. 1987
sentence. LIFE
work. special squad
transferred to
mental health unit
LSP 3. 9. 99

doc # 408678
dob. 7. 27. 74
pob. Bogalusa
sentence. 2 ½ years
3 children
work. road crew
LCIW 7. 13. 00

Joshua Williams Angola, Louisiana

Mary Sumling St. Gabriel, Louisiana

doc # 345191

dob. 1. 14. 76

pob. New Orleans

entered 1994

sentence. LIFE

work. line 5

LSP 4. 22. 99

doc # 311647

dob. 2. 4. 51

pob. Paula, MS

sentence. 10 years

3 children

work. inner yard

Mardi Gras Parade

LCIW 3. 2. 01

Chaunta Laurent St. Gabriel, Louisiana

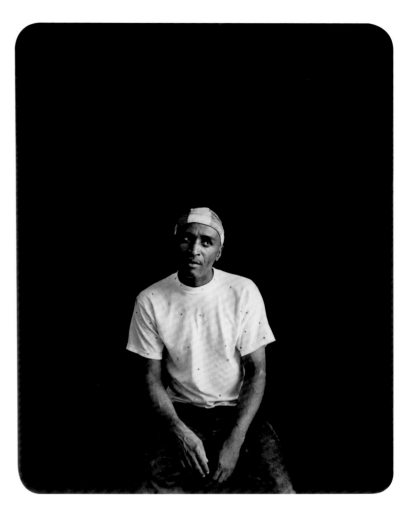

Dan Riley Angola, Louisiana

doc #394489

dob. 9. 18. 78

pob. New Orleans

sentence. 5 years

1 child

work. office occupation

LCIW 7. 12. 00

doc #113138

dob. 6. 23. 50

pob. New Orleans

entered LSP. 1992

sentence. LIFE

work. yard orderly

special squad

LSP 6. 10. 99

Artifact

Self-extinguishing cigarette holder with failsafe tilt ring
patent #4991595 2-12-91 Roscoe Jones #105190

(This way if you're lying back on the couch on a slow night, drinking, sweat-
ing in front of the swamp box, swatting mosquitoes, and you happen to fall off before
the dogs, you won't burn up)

First Memory

Her and her cousin playing house with a cardboard box: grass was greens,
     grasshoppers was meat, mud was bread

Falling off the porch busting open my head, he said as he turned his close-
     shaved skull around on its muscular stalk

     For whatever it's worth
My friend here   her mother was murdered
     sleeping in her own bed
One stepfather shot playing cards
     her college man died on a motorcyle in a foreign land not long after
     they let him out of the bughouse
And mine by his own hand
     with his partner's target pistol

                    Count the days of summer ahead

                    Count the years you finished in school

                    Count the jobs you don't qualify to hold

                    Count the smokes you've got left

                    Count the friends you've got on the inside

                    Count the ones who've already fallen

Why, Good morning Miss Toliver, how are you

My pressure went up on me   If you have sons and daughters
          they cause your pressure to go up
          Come on down to the station and see me Baby
          I got to get back on the air Come on down

En Louisiane

          spit out a seed and up springs a watermelon

The old leprosarium in Carville lost its tax exemption
          during the Reagan years; then the army moved in

          We don't stand for corruption we demand it

Chicken pox can be dried up by scaring chickens
                                        to fly over the afflicted child
En Louisiane
          formosan termites on the wing

          more religion than you can shake a stick at
                                        en Louisiane
Remember Pop lived through his execution
had to let him go   that's the law   *en Louisiane*

In the mind of Joe Christmas
her death not an aberration but an abstraction to him
          brought on by bitchery and abomination

          Found: the doctor's wife
her two-year-old quadruplets crawling around in her blood
unharmed   unharmed   the papers said

Book the good doctor's cell in advance—high season rates

Go home now Pop, this bed is reserved for a predator

This bed now belongs to the good doctor

Bubba's got fresh gar for the senior citizens
None of that old gar Come on down and see
between The Projects and The Sweet Potato Man

In this subtle and savage light...

Wrap this program around the shut-ins and the shut-outs
have a little mercy, etc.

I AM SENTENCED TO DEATH BY ELECTROCUTION!
According to state records, in 1970, 30 years ago. To have electricity
pass through my body until I am pronounced dead. Yes, you heard me
right, I am all stirred up. I am the seventh child to the late Sister Rose
—Aaron

He lived in that big old house   with his dogs   his guns

Was that a harley or a coffin you were driving

Can I take off my tie yet

Keep on rocking in the free world

No we're not parole officers
No we're not church ladies
The redhead here is a photographer and I'm her humble factotum

Dino knows   he's got to be good until he gets off paper

                                                              The sickly ambrosia of hope

church marquee: life fragile
                                                              handle with prayer
the subtle and savage light

        the fecundity   the enstiflement   the hole that dreams

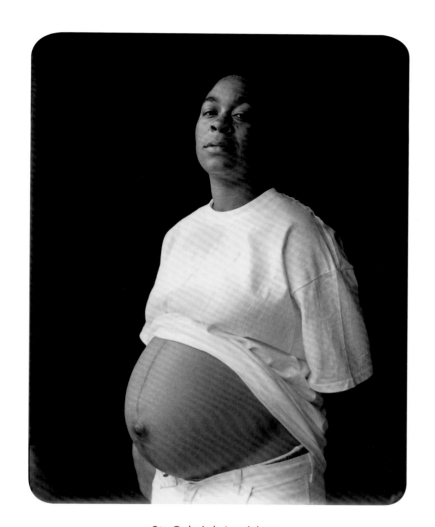

St. Gabriel, Louisiana

St. Gabriel, Louisiana

doc # 350401
dob. 3. 13. 72
pob. New Orleans
sentence. 1 year
1 child
work. housekeeper
LCIW 2. 8. 02

doc # 402710
dob. 2. 13. 53
pob. Florida
sentence. 15 years
1 child
work. library
children's day
Christmas party
LCIW 12. 9. 00

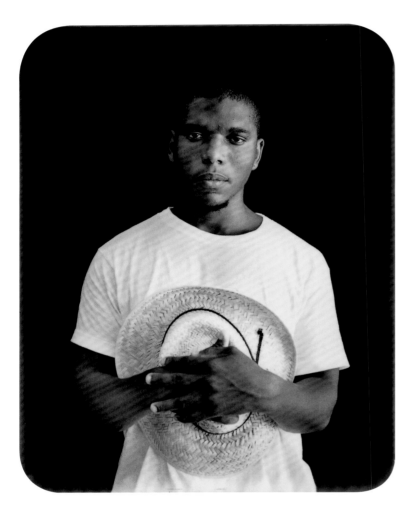

Christopher "Lil' Flex" Pendleton Angola, Louisiana

St. Gabriel, Louisiana

doc #357275
dob. 6. 11. 76
pob. New Orleans
sentence. LIFE
work. field
LSP 6. 10. 99

doc #200003
dob. 1. 25. 47
pob. Sikeston, MO
sentence. 5 years
4 children
work. culinary arts
LCIW 4. 30. 99

Le ciel est par-dessus le toit

the windows here

      whiten in increments

There is no emptiness

only a silence that does not go in reverse

    I want to say I will be there   to collect your tears

after all, I am not Sister Prejean

no one here for urinating in public

    tell me a woman's hand will moisten your lips

      7 a.m., the white ladies already out on soul patrol

Come On Down,

The food is cheap the squirrels are black   you get drive-through daiquiris
at Macdaiquiri Factory   jumbo shrimp for $5.50 lb. at the Sinclair
cataracts removed at Dr. Broussard's pecans at Mayonnaise's Place
50 flavors at the sno-cone shack   and soft soft real soft ice cream
barbecue at Pardners delivered by pony express   cathead biscuits
you can get your smothered steak at Hen House; collards, rhubarb cobbler,
cornbread still sittin' on the side

St. Gabriel, Louisiana

Donna "Sky" Johnson St. Gabriel, Louisiana

doc # 320216
dob. 6. 24. 67
pob. Lafayette
sentence. 3½ years
4 children
work. inner yard
portrait with inner yard
workers' pet toad
LCIW 6. 15. 00

doc # 115195
dob. 4. 30. 59
pob. Oceanside, C A
sentence. 5 years
2 children
work. culinary arts
LCIW 4. 30. 99

Erica Smith St. Gabriel, Louisiana

St. Gabriel, Louisiana

doc # 420949
dob. 9. 22. 81
pob. New Orleans
sentence. 1 year
1 child
work. job skills
education program
LCIW 3. 2. 01

doc # 103565
dob. 12. 26. 48
pob. Lake Charles
sentence. LIFE
work. inner yard
LCIW 11. 30. 99

Teka Kwitha Jefferson St. Gabriel, Louisiana

St. Gabriel, Louisiana

doc # 170126

dob. 4. 30. 62

pob. New Orleans

sentence. 2½ years

2 children

work. culinary arts

LCIW 4. 30. 99

doc # 410525

dob. 6. 26. 78

pob. Lafayette

sentence. 5 years

work. culinary arts

LCIW 4. 14. 00

Michelle Hill St. Gabriel, Louisiana

St. Gabriel, Louisiana

doc # 391637
dob. 12. 27. 67
pob. New Orleans
sentence. 2 ½ years
2 children
work. culinary arts
LCIW 4. 30. 99

doc # 375279
dob. 11. 2. 69
pob. Houston, TX
sentence. 10 years
1 child
work. culinary arts
LCIW 4. 14. 00

Leaving St. Gabriel:

a gift of Mexican heather in a styrofoam cup

Whatever you do   don't pass that sno-cone shack

Carlighter burns on cashier's neck

Think upwards   It's too hot

Why does it take so goddamn long—the burned up years, the landscape memorized without benefit of wheels, the nearly pretty house, the nearly nice room, uneventful days, implausible schemes on the heels of unpreventable nights; the perpetually pissed-off ones who just wanted to hurt somebody, the incipiently pissed who had to be roused with a broom, the well-meaners who tried to help, the feckless risks, the nearly helpful teacher, the failures that can be achieved without trying, the sick bosses, the wrong beds with the wrong ones, the unheeded infections, all the ugly run-over shoes, the thousand stupid things you wanted (others had them); the carcasses of your young dumb dreams strewn all over the slithering hills...

If you could just say I feel lost here and I'm going to go home now. For where on earth would you buy that ticket. Who would meet you when you got there. By what sign would they know you.

A man seated below the copia of mounted heads at The Mohawk said he came from Old Floyd. In the town center of Old Floyd they had a bell that came from France, and when hunters lost themselves in the forest the bell would be rung so they could find their way out. It was, the man said, his dream to lose himself in the forest and be saved by the bell. Saved by the bell. Get it.

A circle of blackened rocks, vagrant moon, the trees that say Come near; the bull that doesn't care...

I who once fled north slumped over the pew of a family of prominence and came back with my glasses taped at the stem (as a dog returneth to his vomit).

Longing to touch the unguarded earth, touch it while it is still warm.

Recurrent dream of freedom: you are outside. It rains. The water turns you transparent and sexual—like electricity caught in a jar. Suddenly you are wide awake and everything you ever wanted is here. You will never need gloves again, never be out-of-date. Harm or be harmed, take or be taken. You can cry and creature here. So quietly can you die.

Then the images are upside down, inside out. After typing your entire life, you discover your carbons are in backwards. Where there should be darkness, the light is hard on and vice versa. Except for that long blue rag of land. And the white pelicans on Sugar Lake.

Up north with its thirty minutes in the sun, good schools for the moneyed and silent alarms, and south with its petrochemical plants and joblessness. And the children of children, buckets of children, jumping through snatches of smoke, penitentiary bound.

Barred from both and you miss them terribly.

Linked to an experience a feeling deep down
that won't stop twisting   until the last rivet of grief is secure

All our days are numbered. Not unlike old lumber for a house that's going to be moved and lived in all over again. Same old blunders on a different hill.

And you, only a number.

Not a fresh fish anymore.

Got a face on you.

Not a part of, apart from.

Cropped out of the picture.

Vice Versa.

Termaine Deon "T.C." Cunningham Transylvania, Louisiana

doc # 396684
dob. 2. 12. 78
pob. Shreveport
sentence. 5 years
ECPPF 1999

Franklin Jones Angola, Louisiana

doc # 82954
dob. 11. 17. 39
pob. Woodville, TX
entered LSP. 1972
sentence. LIFE
work. cell block orderly
LSP 6. 10. 99

St. Gabriel, Louisiana

doc # 421166
dob. 10. 20. 76
pob. Baton Rouge
sentence. 7 years
1 child
work. inner yard
LCIW 6. 15. 00

Rhonda Payne St. Gabriel, Louisiana

Angola, Louisiana

doc # 333265

dob. 11. 17. 71

pob. New Orleans

sentence. 10 years

3 children

work. chair factory

LCIW 6. 25. 99

doc # 331625

dob. 8. 8. 75

pob. New Orleans

entered LSP. 1994

sentence. LIFE

work. recreation orderly

LSP 4. 22. 99

Tina McGee St. Gabriel, Louisiana

George Meche Angola, Louisiana

doc # 384946
dob. 6. 25. 76
pob. New Orleans
sentence. 15 years
work. inner yard
tattoo. mo dollars
mo problems
LCIW 7. 12. 00

doc # 94808
dob. 8-18-59
pob. Crowley
entered LSP. 1995
sentence. LIFE
work. line 25
LSP 9. 17. 99

Shawn Foster Angola, Louisiana

Herald "Bubba Brand" Brand Angola, Louisiana
Kenneth "Buddy" Woodburn, Jr. Angola, Louisiana

doc # 360526
dob. 2. 20. 78
pob. Houston, TX
entered LSP. 1993
sentence. LIFE
work. line 1
rodeo events.
bulldoggin',
buddy pickup
LSP 10. 31. 99

doc # 334956
dob. 6. 11. 72
pob. Picayune, MS
entered LSP. 1993
sentence. LIFE
work. New Orleans
Baptist Theological
Seminary
rodeo events.
bulldoggin'

doc # 330091
dob. 11. 23. 73
pob. Kenner
entered LSP. 1993
sentence. LIFE
work. New Orleans
Baptist Theological
Seminary
rodeo events.
bronc & bull riding,
wild horse race
LSP 10. 31. 99

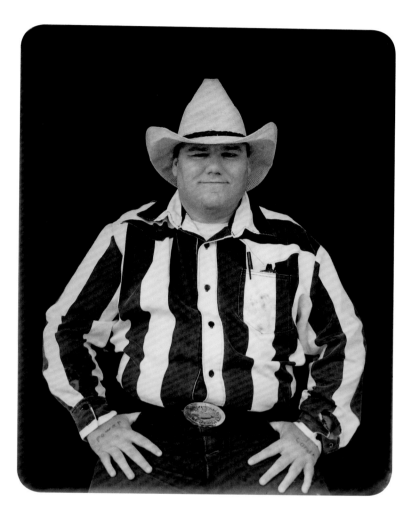

Harry Kersey Angola, Louisiana

Robin Forgette St. Gabriel, Louisiana

doc # 359847
dob. 10.13.54
pob. Indianapolis, IN
entered LSP. 1996
sentence. LIFE
work. yard
rodeo events.
bulldoggin',
convict poker
LSP 10.31.99

doc # 132340
dob. 1.19.49
pob. Houston, TX
1 child
work. big laundry
Mardi Gras Parade
LCIW 3.2.01

Just Another Day

at the iron pile

Hotter said the inmate   between sets
than my thirteen-year-old niece

Squats 600
Benches 450

One young man patiently braids
the head of another

When I said I lived in New England
he asked if I ever saw Princess Diana

Body Language

What does that tattoo say
That's my baby's name
What is your baby's name
UTOPIA

Is this the tattoo that says Utopia,
No, this is the tattoo that says Real Men Eat Pussy

I could have told you not to ask

Jugged her jugular

The jury's collective shudder

You behave, he told her, before he cut her neck

It is not alone the meaning of sorrow and its beauty
but the ongoingness of things that so impresses me
The old dirty-word tattoos are blotted over by a blur of birds

At the death row spiritual seminar banquet
        the men shackled just at the ankles
And to look around the room at all the families at table
        It could be anywhere

Yes, there's a woman on the row
        I recall   she did her partner
And I don't remember who else
        When she walks   the yard is cleared

Delivered the long-awaited letter
        setting date and time of execution
to the wrong damned man
        I shit you not

Come nearer   there is no emptiness

Yes it's bitter   every bit of it bitter

Day is long

The night will pass

With or without the rain

We need so badly

Gloria Wesley St. Gabriel, Louisiana

doc # 365866

dob. 10. 10. 61

pob. Monroe

sentence. 20 years

6 children

LCIW 6. 25. 99

Eddie M. "Fat" Coco Transylvania, Louisiana

doc # 409584
dob. 6. 30. 79
pob. New Orleans
sentence. 6 years
2 children
future plans.
be success, lawyer
ECPPF 3. 8. 02

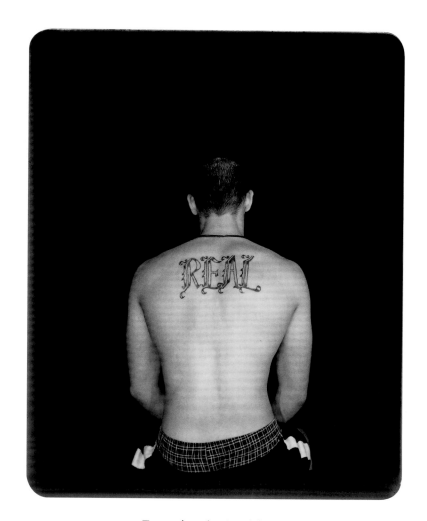

Transylvania, Louisiana

transferred to
Hunt Prison
Boot Camp

Dear Child of God,

If you will allow me time.   To make a dove.   I will spend it
well.   A half success is more than can be hoped for.   And
turning on the hope machine is dangerous to contemplate   First.
I have to find a solid bottom.   Where the scum gets hard and
the scutwork starts.   One requires ideal tools: a huge suitcase
            of love   a set of de-iced wings   the ghost of a flea
Music intermittent or ongoing.   Here.   One exits the forest
of men and women.   Here.   One re-dreams the big blown dream
of socialism.   Deep in the suckhole.   Where Lou Vindie kept
her hammer.   Under her pillow.   Like a wedge of wedding cake.
Working from my best memory.   Of a bird I first saw nesting.

                                    In the razor wire.

Lines of Defense including Proceedings from the State of Louisiane

vs.

The Convergence of the Ur-real and the Unreal

Q: Where were you on the night in question

A: Watching re-runs

Q: What did you do before

A: Fattened frogs for snakes

Q: Before that

A: Sold monkeys door to door

Q: Did you ever imagine yourself doing something really useful

A: N/A

Q: What's your DOC#

Q: What's your idea of Love, Loss, Mercy, etc.

A: N/A

Q: What can you tell us about your passenger

A: She was a slab of a woman, Your Honor

Q: Which is sadder a motel or a public john

Q: When did your troubles with the revenue service begin

A: On Kafka's birthday, Your Honor

Q: How many prisons have we passed

A: Just four

Q: Was that a harley or a coffin you were driving

Q: Is that the tattoo that says UTOPIA

A: No, that's the tattoo that says Real Men Eat Pussy

Q: What do you call a flesh wound

A: About the thickness of a pair of panties, Your Honor

Wilbert Jones Angola, Louisiana

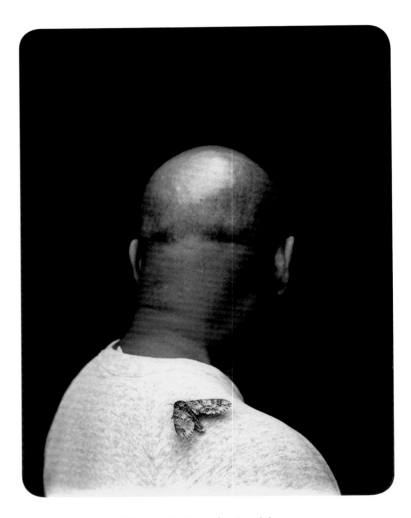

"Count" Angola, Louisiana

doc #80949
dob. 10. 1. 52
pob. New Orleans
entered LSP. 1976
sentence. LIFE
work. kitchen
LSP 3. 19. 99

doc #62167
dob. 2. 12. 41
pob. New Orleans
entered LSP. 1959
sentence. LIFE
work. kitchen
LSP 3. 19. 99

"Brother C.J." Angola, Louisiana

doc #22237
dob. 6. 29. 58
pob. New Orleans
entered LSP. 1993
sentence. LIFE
work. close custody
restriction tier walker
necklace with
photograph
of grandchild
LSP 4. 22. 99

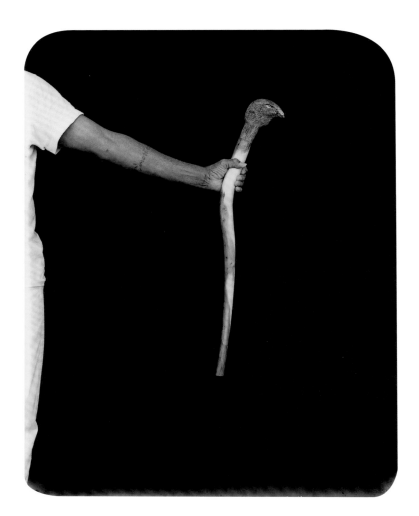

Phillip Ray Allen Angola, Louisiana

"Barbara" by Johnny "Ray Boy" Madison
Transylvania, Louisiana

doc # 74672

doc # 102499

dob. 2. 5. 39

dob. 11. 2. 62

pob. Rayville

pob. Monroe

entered LSP. 1973

sentence. 10 years

sentence. LIFE

matchstick sailing ship

4 children

ECPPF 6. 3. 00

work. kitchen

tattoo. Mother

wood carver

since 1975

LSP 2. 24. 99

Kenny Smith Transylvania, Louisiana

Little Lamb by Sherral Kahey St. Gabriel, Louisiana

doc # 111222
dob. 7. 20. 59
pob. Baltimore, Maryland
sentence. 18 months
ECPPF 1999

doc # 102507
dob. 7. 13. 48
pob. Austin, TX
sentence. LIFE
5 children
8 grandchildren
work. literacy tutor
LCIW 4. 15. 00

Q: Westinghoused or edisoned, your choice
       AC or DC
A: It's no real pleasure in life

Q: Did you have any pets
A: I kept a dog

Q: How did you get rid of the stains
A: I know hot water sets blood

Q: How do you get rid of dirty chi
A: Ask Jeeves

Q: Do you believe in progress
A: See the black curl under my chin
       I live on the ground by day and by night…

Q: Whom do you see in the mirror,
       What is your favorite body of water, and why
       What is your idea of a good car
       Do you like fried pickles
       How long were you in school, what was your favorite subject
       How old were you when you began to mutilate yourself
       What is the nicest thing anyone ever did for you
       Did you ever have your own room
       Did you wet the bed
       Did you pour salt on slugs
       Did he touch you there
       Did you ever make anyone something you were proud of
       Can you carry a tune
       Do you like okra
       Have you ever been scared to the core

Q: What did she say
A: Say, Your Honor,   she say oh my godohmygodohmygod
       Say, Your Honor,   she say oh honey ohhoneyohhoneyno

Count her bruises and contusions

Count the baby's teeth

Count your bills

Count the birds you bagged

Count the pups Sissy had

Count the shots fired

Count the puncture wounds

Count your cavities

Count the years

Friend, Did you happen to violate the law. Did you get a murder ticket. Did you do dope all night. Did you rob the convenience grocery store and steal my daughter's car. Are you so worried you just don't know which way to turn. I recommend you turn to Amco Bail and Bond. Just call Ditty Bop. He'll be there in ten or fifteen minutes. Don't sit around at the P farm with your feet all swole up, splitting open, and running over. Pick up the phone. Soon as Mr. Ditty Bop picks up his hat and coat, he's ready to go.

Why not check it out and lock it down

We're moving on my Christian friends,
We're moving on into

Difficult to look at the woman

much less photograph   and not ask
about a scar that runs from one ear
        to the opposing breast

        whose babies died of smoke inhalation

Or the gasoline-wrecked face
of the green-eyed black man

her grease-splotched back and shoulders

Or the tattooed likeness of dead Elena
        on her sister's forearm

        Mo dollars   Mo problems

        says the other forearm

The wrist lashed with paint chips once everything else
        removed from the cell

Or the one who ate the tv antenna

Her tattered ear; the totaled eyes of the woman who no longer
        knows a soul living on the other side

        Just came down for Mardi Gras

                                        Dialed her mother's number
though she had not seen the woman in thirty years and knew full well
                        her mother passed

                Tuesday's just as bad

The guileless face of the one whose boyfriend beat her lastingly senseless

        Who told us her Auntie lived in Monroe but had to go
        because her house was possessed; at first the spirit was kind
        made her pots of coffee, dusted the furniture...

Wednesdays were important for Faith

No up or down

Grew up in Waterproof
Grew up chasing chickens in Waterproof, Louisiana

I am down for life she said   with a near smile
I've been down for eighteen years

Eddie M. "Fat" Coco, Jr. Transylvania, Louisiana

Dane Donley Transylvania, Louisiana

doc # 409584
dob. 6. 30. 79
pob. New Orleans
sentence. 6 years
2 children
future plans.
be success,
lawyer

Antonio "Small" Coco
dob. 10. 31. 80
pob. New Orleans
sentence. 3 years
future plans.
stay out of trouble
ECPPF 7. 15. 00

doc # 390393
dob. 10. 9. 78
pob. Metarie
sentence. 5 years
tattoo.
Foolish
ECPPF 2000

Tracy "Pick" Horne Angola, Louisiana

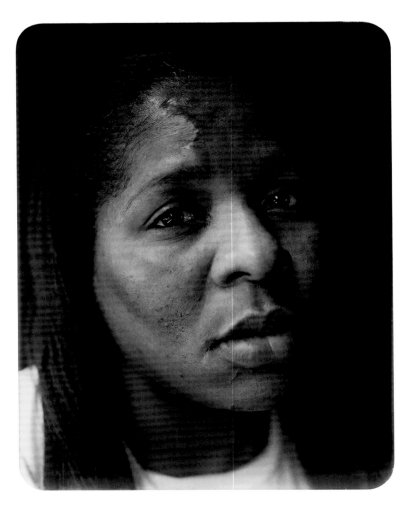

Marcella Lewis St. Gabriel, Louisiana

doc # 131729

dob. 12. 21. 65

pob. Monroe

entered LSP. 1998

sentence.

2 years 7 months

work. special squad

LSP 6. 11. 99

doc #185230

dob. 9. 8. 63

pob. Farmerville

sentence. 35 years

3 children

work. garment factory

LCIW 7. 12. 00

John "K Dog" Edwards Angola, Louisiana

doc # 389602

dob. 1. 7. 79

pob. Baton Rouge

entered LSP. 1998

sentence. 20 years

work. hospital orderly

born without

sweat glands

LSP 3. 18. 99

Wearing that stand-by-the-door dress
with her near smile

I'm a budget person   and a night person, a Cancer

I miss the moon   My aunt raised me

She was a budget person   When she passed

 I began to do the blues unlimited   hard time

        In the ascending order of your feelings

on Moh's Scale of Hardness it's a ten

        It's a cold cold real cold feeling

Every morning she started with a cup of black coffee   a Pall Mall
        and a spiral notebook

It was November   the room darkened
And Mother said   Don't turn the light on
        Cookie she called me

        Phrases saved like pieces of string

She was only 28
        cropped out of the picture

I know Nolan's daddy died of rabbit fever

                                        before he had a face on him

After inspecting the ventilation came down with gaol fever

        Phrases saved like parts of old machinery

I know Bubba fishes all night
        to bring you fresh gar and fresh goo for the senior citizens
                                        none of that old gar or goo

Robert Earl "June" Lewis Angola, Louisiana

Angela West St. Gabriel, Louisiana

doc # 98335

doc # 348804

dob. 9. 30. 60

dob. 4. 2. 68

pob. Slidell

pob. Ohio

sentence. LIFE

sentence. 14 years

work. barber shop

work. chair factory

LSP 6. 10. 99

LCIW 6. 25. 99

En Louisiane   we don't stand for corruption   we demand it

    cathead biscuits fresh gar none of that old gar fried pickles lima beans
                                          hypocrite pie still sittin' on the side

    then her aunt got tired of it so she cursed the spirit; then it got mean;
    whenever her aunt came back in the room the cross would be upside down;

    What do you know
The good governor has issued a proclamation
    asking Louisianans to pray for rain

After the Housefire

    Count your children

    Count them again

    Count the reasons why you came into being in the first place

    Count your nickels

    Count the days you've got left before your next check

    Count the staples in the back of your head

    Count the wrong turns you took to get here

    When the spirit entered her cousin it left cuts on his chest that said F --- you;
    then he went to school and drew a ouija board on the chalkboard and T H E
    E Y E M O V E D; then her aunt had a big vase and the spirit cut it dead in half
    no crumbs or nothing;

He should have never dropped out of 4-H
Improves   head   heart   hands

What's your D O C #

Weapon of Opportunity

He used a dirk
a dirk is a dagger

He used a bezoar
a bezoar is undigested matter from a cow's gut

I shit you not

Ladies and Gentlemen of the Jury,
        Is this your true verdict.
        What say you one and all.

Count the nights you lay awake waiting

Count the nights you lay awake wondering

Count the ways you re-wrote the ending

Landing on PRISON or RUIN send the player's piece
Back to begin life over again from Space No. 1.
I can't make this right *It is ungettable*
in the blank space for future plans he wrote *barker*

Fried pickles: another discordant culinary experience

Snake-infested dreams at the heel of the Tunica hills

        Shift   into absence

Often picture   in my mind's eye   the light on Sugar Lake
        the loft of white pelicans from the cypress stand

None but employee or trusty or fugitive
        has seized the sun going down there

Angola, Louisiana

doc # 107786
dob. 7. 19. 25
pob. Liberty, MS
entered LSP. 1983
sentence. LIFE
no duty
LSP 3. 18. 00
hospital

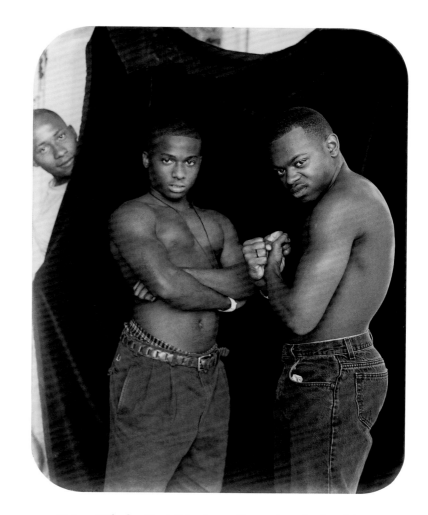

James "Shake Back" Jackson Transylvania, Louisiana

doc # 130457
dob. 8.11.68
pob. Monroe
sentence. 8 years

Quinn "Kareem"
Millage
doc # 474847
dob. 8.25.81
pob. Jonesboro
future plans.
psychologist

Brian "Lil' Collins"
Jackson
dob. 2.6.79
pob. Ruston
sentence. 8 years
future plans.
own a barber
shop
ECPPF 1999

James "Shake Back" Jackson Transylvania, Louisiana

"R J" Transylvania, Louisiana

doc #130457
dob. 8. 11. 68
pob. Monroe
sentence. 8 years
ECPPF 1999

dob. 4. 8. 53
pob. Shreveport
sentence. 2 years
ECPPF 1998

Antonio "Small" Coco Transylvania, Louisiana

Transylvania, Louisiana

doc #407688
dob. 10.31.80
pob. New Orleans
sentence. 3 years
future plans.
stay out of trouble
ECPPF 6.1.00

ECPPF 1998

See the black curl under my chin
I live on the ground by day and by night...
                                        Don't ask

Whom do you see in the mirror

A flick of the conscience
        before the windows darken in hard vertical lines

It is inenarrable

A trunkful of snake-infested dreams

The grey pelican is the state bird

Her aunt moved from Ruby to Florence
because her house was possessed
                                Don't ask
        The you that you fear
                                is here

The fear that you fear is everywhere

Emotional collision of taker and taken

        Hot water sets blood

Helluva lot easier to kill than pass a bad check

Imagine if it were your son

        Badly decomposed

        Coffin kept closed

The strapdown team is strictly voluntary
        you would be there

An area man tried to describe
        the sanctity of being
        a state very like happiness

ODI ET AMO   don't we all

Hate bracketed by love

Vice versa

AMA guidelines forbid a physician to be a participant

The pavid eyes the gravid set to the jaw of the condemned

      see me   hear me   feel me

I go I go at last I go — his face transfiguring

      THE EYE MOVED

      memory extinguished

      let no man remember my name

      Mercy Triumphs over Judgment
        easy for some to say

barely imaginable rage   unimaginable grief   unthinkable deed

No messenger from the czar on a foaming white horse
      to return the air to you

      Old Fyodor was a real mess after that one

Job applicant in the waiting room said the best way was to
      treat them all like a #

      That could be a problem, Stupid

That crime which dare not speak its name
      (oft confused with unjudicial conduct)

Whoever FIRST arrives at The Mansion of Happiness
      WINS THE GAME.

This must be reached by exact spin

Kenton Matthews Transylvania, Louisiana

doc # 117452

dob. 8. 7. 66

pob. Chicago, IL

sentence. 3 years

4 children

future plans.

computer data entry

E C P P F 3. 15. 00

Zack K. Oakes Transylvania, Louisiana

dob. 9. 20. 73
pob. Shreveport
sentence. 5 years
ECPPF 1998

Antoinette Ford St. Gabriel, Louisiana

Jeff Todd Transylvania, Louisiana

doc # 412541

dob. 7. 31. 79

pob. Oakland, CA

sentence. 5 years 4 months

work. incarcerated

LCIW 6. 15. 00

doc # 0399745

dob. 11. 25. 79

pob. East Carroll Parish

sentence. 2 years

ECPPF 1999

Enters a silence that never reverses itself

                                        What was he reading

                                        i/m preferred not to speak to the press

                                        i/m preferred not to eat with the warden

                                        i/m preferred to see his own pastor

                                        i/m asked that his mother not be present

                                        i/m asked that his eyes be given to another

Today it's going to be hot as blue blazes
And tonight it will be very very warm
Tomorrow it's going to be hot as blue blazes
And tomorrow night it will be very very warm

Tuesday's just as bad

We must rest now; it's going to be a scorcher

Before you know it the sun is coming up and everything is moving clockwise
                                        is your blood headed in the right direction

Dear Errant Kid,

    Remember the almighty finger on the wrong answer button.

Dear Damned Doomed and Forgotten,

    Mother Helen has a bad feeling — the rehearsals for your execution
have already begun.

Dear Fugitive,

    No one's beat the dogs yet.

Dear Virtual Lifer,

    This is strictly a what if proposition:
What if I were to trade my manumission for your incarceration. If only for a day.
At the end of which the shoes must be left at the main gate to be filled by their original occupants. There is no point and we will not shrink from it. There is only this
day to re-invent everything and lose it all over again. Nothing will be settled or
made easy.

    PS: Difference Between Natural and Virtual Lifer :
I can't do ninety-nine years even on the installment plan —
    The Last Heel Stringer d. 1999, aged 71
    Natural lifer   Don't even ask

St. Gabriel, Louisiana

"Shot Gun" Angola, Louisiana

doc # 400858
dob. 9. 3. 62
pob. New Orleans
sentence. LIFE
4 children
work. tutor
Halloween
haunted house
LCIW 10. 27. 00

doc # 293093
dob. 6. 11. 64
entered LSP. 1995
sentence.
11 years 9 months
work. field
LSP 3. 4. 99

Larry Gregory Transylvania, Louisiana

Isaac "No Limit" Bella Transylvania, Louisiana

doc # 350435

dob. 12. 10. 76

pob. Monroe

sentence. 2 years

ECPPF 1999

doc # 399270

dob. 6. 15. 78

pob. New Orleans

sentence. 4 years

ECPPF 1999

Your Honor,
          these are but a few impressions of pain

Now you talk I'm losing my voice

It does get old

If you change your mind let me know

Up yours

I'm in the book

What if it's the guns, Stupid

The way we do things

These are only words   you too have penitentiary potential

We may meet in a steel mirror
          behind rows of amaranthus and vortices of razor wire

What are you looking at screamed the perp's sister
          after the verdict was in

          kicking the tires of the victim's kin

How do you get rid of dirty chi
          Once and for all
          Ask Jeeves

A case of late-afternoon hysterics

Hopelessness against hopelessness

A woman is better in the gun tower than a man
less hesitant   they say   to shoot a man on the run

Think upwards

It's too hot

One last word:

St. Gabriel, Louisiana

doc # 200713
dob. 7. 9. 53
pob. Waterproof
sentence. 33 years
4 children
work. inner yard
LCIW 10. 26. 00

Raymond Guidry Angola, Louisiana

"Speedy" Angola, Louisiana

doc # 102952
doc. 1. 18. 52
pob. Lafayette
entered LSP. 1984
sentence. LIFE
rodeo events. 3
LSP 10. 31. 99

doc # 76070
dob. 4. 21. 47
pob. Seymour, IN
entered LSP. 1971
sentence. LIFE
work. tractor repair
LSP 2. 24. 99

"K's Kitty" St. Gabriel, Louisiana

doc # 115082
dob. 4. 26. 57
pob. Amarillo, TX
sentence. 5 years
4 children
work. outer perimeter
LCIW 7. 13. 00

NO ONE NO BODY IS BAD FOREVER

Aaron don't proclaim foresight

It's 99° at 7:54 the real feel temperature is 114°

the Jewel of the Dial is next

Can I take off my tie yet

Do you want to
        shut down   sleep   restart

It gets old
The way we do things

I am all stirred up

And so, I took out her tintypes

                                    And drew the prisoners around me

Legend

ECPPF   East Carroll Parish Prison Farm (Transylvania, Louisiana)
minimum security for men

LCIW   Louisiana Correctional Institute for Women
(St. Gabriel, Louisiana)
minimum, medium, and maximum security for women

LSP   Louisiana State Penitentiary (Angola, Louisiana)
maximum security for men

DOC   Department of Corrections Number

DOB   Date of Birth

POB   Place of Birth

Work. Current prison work assignment.

The larger inmate populations of the LSP and the LCIW allow for a greater variety of work, skill-training, activities, and organizations. Future Plans were most often provided at the ECPPF because the terms are short enough to imagine a future beyond incarceration. The lines in italics describe the wording of tattoos. The final date listed indicates when the photograph was taken. A few of the inmates requested their names be withheld, and some provided only their nicknames. The men photographed in large stripes are participants in the annual rodeo at Angola. In Louisiana, both Halloween and Mardi Gras are celebrated in extravagantly imaginative ways at the LCIW, which is why a number of the women have posed in costume.

Note: The variation in the kind of information given is due in part to the sheer press of circumstances during the photo sessions, and in part due to particular notations or omissions by the inmates. Also, the forms provided inmates were somewhat different in makeup from institution to institution, which is why the women generally listed the number of children they had, and the men only occasionally noted children.

The information provided by the inmates is etched on the backs of the original metal photographic plates.

IN MEMORY OF

Mary Elizabeth Pyeatt Gunter
1911—1986

and

Jean Alryn Gunter Tovrea
Murdered
Good Friday, April 1, 1988

The aim is not to connect particular perpetrators to particular victims but to convey a cultural landscape of violent activity, its consequences, its toll. This is clearly not a systematic document but one photographer's and one poet's unreserved, subjective views of an American institution, indeed, an American phenomenon.

Why not check it out and lock it down:

In the Belly of the Beast (Abbott), My Return (Abbott), The Evidence of Things Not Seen (Baldwin), Book of Evidence (Banville), Waiting for Godot (Beckett), God of the Rodeo (Bergner), False Starts (Braly), On the Yard (Braly), Last Man In (Braun), Dying to Tell (Butler and Henderson), Angola: Louisiana State Penitentiary, A Half-Century of Rage and Reform (Butler and Henderson), #85 Catullus, The Stranger (Camus), In Cold Blood (Capote), Sleepers (Carcaterra), The Falconer (Cheever), The Blue Book of Crime (Cooke), The House of the Dead (Dostoyevsky), The Count of Monte Cristo (Dumas), Death Watch (Foster), Discipline and Punish (Foucault), Prison Writing in 20th Century America (Franklin, ed.), Thief's Journal (Genet), Our Lady of the Flowers (Genet), The Bend, The Lip, the Kid (Gordon), Prison Notebooks (Gramsci), Prison Letters (Gramsci), Wake Up Dead Man (Jackson, ed.), Killing Time (Jackson), Final Exposure (Jones and Savel), The Trial (Kafka), The Castle (Kafka), "The Penal Colony" (Kafka), Shawshank Redemption (King), Photography, Vision, and the Production of Modern Bodies (Lalvani), Texas Death Row (Light and Donovan), Conversations with the Dead (Lyon), The Executioner's Song (Mailer), Fable of the Bees (Mandeville), Osip Mandelstam: Selected Poems (Brown and Merwin, transl.), Vernooykill Creek (Matlin), Race to Incarcerate (Mauer), The Captive Mind (Milosz), The Oxford History of the Prison (Morris and Rothman, eds.), "A Good Man Is Hard To Find," (O'Connor), My Life Is My Sun Dance (Peltier), Dead Man Walking (Prejean), The Angolite (Wilbert Rideau, ed.), The Discovery of the Asylum (Rothman), No Exit (Sartre), Charterhouse of Parma (Stendhal), Cells of Release (Templeton), Prisoner without a Name, Cell Without a Number (Timerman), "Le ciel est par-dessus le toit" (Verlaine), Brothers and Keepers (Wideman), De Profundis (Wilde), "The Ballad of Reading Gaol" (Wilde), and Sister Pearlee Toliver, the Jewel of the Dial. She's an innovator, a motivator, an inspirator, a generator; never a spectator, and always on the cutting edge of gospel music. KYEA 98.3

Note: The Mansion of Happiness was the first board game published in America, An Instructive Moral and Entertaining Amusement, invented by Miss Abbott, the daughter of a Beerly, Massachusetts, clergyman, and first published in Salem, Massachusetts, by the old book firm of W. & S.B. Ives, 1843, republished in its original form by Parker Brothers Inc. in response to many requests, 1926.

Acknowledgments

With thanks for access permission and patient support to Warden Burl Cain and his staff and to Classification Officer Gary Young at Louisiana State Penitentiary; Warden Johnnie W. Jones, Deputy Warden Linda Guidroz, Education Coordinator Michael Heath, and the staff of the Louisiana Correctional Institute for Women; and to Warden Edward Knight and his staff and to Warden Alfred McDaniels at the East Carroll Parish Prison Farm.

And with special gratitude to Cathy Fontenot, Director of Classifications (Louisiana State Penitentiary), Assistant Warden Helen Travis, and Literacy Instructor Madeline McCaleb (Louisiana Correctional Institute for Women) for their interest, energy, and example during the time we spent at their institutions. And to former Warden Ray Dixon (East Carroll Parish Prison Farm) for the warm welcome extended by him at the inception of this project.

Special thanks for the courtesy and cooperation of Marianne Fisher-Giorlando (Professor of Criminal Justice at Grambling State University), Burk Foster (Professor, University of Louisiana, Lafayette), and Betty Cole (Director, Tulane Criminal Law Clinic).

With gratitude to the inmates of the Louisiana Correctional Institute for Women, the East Carroll Parish Prison Farm, and the Louisiana State Penitentiary for their trust, participation, conversations, and correspondence.

Also with gratitude to the Center for Documentary Studies at Duke University for the Dorothea Lange-Paul Taylor Prize, which was of great help to this collaboration. And to the Louisiana Endowment for the Humanities, a state affiliate of the National Endowment for the Humanities, for their generous publication grant.

Deborah Luster and C.D. Wright would like to thank the editors of the following publications in which selections of the text and photographs first appeared: BRICK, Conjunctions, Crossroads, Jacket, Jubilat (text only), turnrow, Spot, Louisiana

Cultural Vistas, and *The Tenth Dorothea Lange-Paul Taylor Prize: Deborah Luster and C.D. Wright in Collaboration*, a chapbook produced by the Center for Documentary Studies at Duke University.

The photographer wishes to thank the Bucksbaum Family Award for American Photography, the Friends of Photography, the John Gutmann Photography Fellowship, the San Francisco Foundation, the Anonymous Was a Woman Foundation, the Light Factory, and the Louisiana Division of the Arts.

With gratitude to Kevin Kennedy for counsel and support throughout this project. To my studio assistants over the course of this project— Clarke and Christy Galusha, Tirzah Rose, and Seth Harris. And to Eileen Wallace.

The poet wishes to thank the Lannan Foundation for a 1999 Literary Award, which advanced the development of *One Big Self,* and a month-long residency in Marfa, Texas, in the summer of 2003 which facilitated a final review of the manuscript in production. And to the Foundation for Contemporary Performance Arts for a supporting grant during the period in which this work was written.

Thanks also to the following people for their support of and assistance with this project: Judy Norrell, Merry Foresta, Sandra Phillips, Catherine Edelman, Michael Sartisky, Susan Friedewald, Glenn and April Bucksbaum, Iris Tillman-Hill, Barbara Bloemink, Annie Talbot, Mary Howell, Ben Sandmel, John Hardy, Robert Hennessey, Ray Meeks, Josephine Sacabo, the META Museum, Axel Ziegler, Detective Ed Reynolds, District Attorneys Paul Ahler and Bill Culbertson. To Forrest and Brecht Gander. To Billy Tickle. To Lila Luster. And to Mike Luster.

And many thanks to Jack Woody.

A portion of image plate sales from *One Big Self: Prisoners of Louisiana* is donated to the Inmate Welfare Fund of the represented prison.

Tina McGee St. Gabriel, Louisiana

doc # 384946
dob. 6. 25. 76
pob. New Orleans
sentence. 15 years
work. inner yard

tattoo. portrait of
inmate's sister,
Elena McGee,
murdered in 1994
in a drive-by
shooting at the
St. Bernard Projects,
New Orleans
LCIW 7. 12. 00

Colophon

This first edition of *One Big Self* is limited to 2,000 copies. The photographs and *The Reappearance of Those Who Have Gone* are copyright Deborah Luster, 2003. The text is copyright C.D. Wright, 2003. The contents of this book are copyright Twin Palms Publishers, 2003. This book was printed and bound in China.

Book design is by Jack Woody and Arlyn Eve Nathan. Production management is by Axel Ziegler. The typefaces selected are Frutiger and Requiem.

ISBN 1-931885-25-7

TWIN PALMS PUBLISHERS
Post Office 10229   Santa Fe, NM 87504   1-800-797-0680   www.twinpalms.com

"Old Sparky" Angola, Louisiana

Convict-built replica. From August 1941 through June 1957 Old Sparky was transported by pickup truck to Louisiana's parishes for executions.

From July 1957 to the present, all executions in Louisiana have been performed at Angola Prison.

Lethal injection was adopted by the State in 1991. LSP 6. 24. 99 Red Hat House